My Hedgehog and Me

Merlyn Horn

My Hedgehog and Me

by

Merlyn Horn

NEW MILLENNIUM

310 KENNINGTON ROAD LONDON SE11 4LD

Photographs by the author
Cover photograph by Gordon Lockie

Printed and bound by B.W.D. Northolt, Middx.
Issued by New Millennium*
ISBN 1 85845 023 3
*An imprint of The Professional Authors' & Publishers' Association

For my husband, Ian,
and daughter, Lucy,
with love.

And in memory of good old
'Digger',
who died very peacefully, aged 17,
just before this little book
went to print.

Contents

Page

Introduction by David Bellamy   ix

Chapter I   'Meet Michael Heselspine'   1

Chapter II   'More of Me'   17

Chapter III   'Back to Matters Prickly'   47

Chapter IV   'The Best of Breeds'   67

Chapter V   'All Sorts of Things'   81

Introduction

Of all Britain's wild animals the hedgehog is the one with which most of us come into closest contact. That unmistakable snuffle at the kitchen door that tells us the warm days are here again, coaxing even the most dyed-in-the-wool 'townie' out from beyond the double glazing; that shriek of anguish from the car-bound family as something appears in the beam of the headlights ("Dad, how *could* you?"); that plate of dog's meat, not bread and milk, ideal for a growing family, is cleaned up regular as clockwork, especially as Autumn approachs.

What is so fascinating about a ball of spines and fleas? Read all about it in *My Hedgehog and Me*. Until I read the adventures of Michael Heselspine, I thought it was only the English who were potty about animals!

David Bellamy
Bedburn 1994

Chapter 1

My Hedgehog and Me

'H.I.T.!' I yelled, bringing the car to a grinding halt. 'Oh Lord, not another *Erinaceus europaeus*," sighed my husband Ian, who had once taught Latin in a boys' prep school and who occasionally lapsed into the classical vernacular in times of stress. On this occasion the stress was triggered off by the fact that it was past midnight on a bitterly cold night in late October, and we were on our way home from a particularly tiresome dinner party. Despite being, on the whole, good-natured where my various animals were concerned, all Ian needed at this time of night was an encounter with a defenceless heap of shivering prickles parked right in the middle of the road.

Hence my squawk of 'H.I.T.', which in our family translates as 'hedgehog in trouble'.

'Drat you, why aren't you all curled up in bed like most other self-respecting members of your race?' I muttered rather uncharitably as I clambered out of the car into the icy air and teetered towards the prickly bundle on my hideously uncomfortable, seldom worn, dinner-party high heels. To my surprise, the hedgehog made no effort to curl up into the usual protective ball as would normally be the case when approached by a noisy human in tight high heels, or very bright car headlights heading straight in his direction. This little chap was fully uncurled, and now sat regarding me with beady eyes, his nose swivelling.

Hedgehogs have poor eyesight and are colour-blind, but their senses of smell and hearing are acute, and they are extremely

1

sensitive to sudden sound and movement. The very fact that this hedgehog did not curl up, despite my obvious approach, intrigued me, while alerting me to the strong possibility that all was not well.

'Are you O.K., little chap?' I enquired, while knowing this to be a somewhat stupid question, for it was blatantly obvious even to a non-hedgehog person that he wasn't. The sound of my voice close to his ear produced no reaction, not even a slight defensive stiffening of the prickles, so slowly I reached out and very gently picked him up.

The hedgehog was very small, very cold, very damp, and though apparently uninjured, decidedly dicky on his pins. He also seemed totally un-taken aback at being picked up and handled. Carefully I tucked him into the front of the simulated fur jacket I usually trotted out for posher nocturnal jaunts, and headed back to the car where Ian was sitting, a resigned expression on his face, observing proceedings, and listening appropriately enough to the second movement of Beethoven's Pastoral Symphony on the car radio.

Ian had moved over into the driver's seat, having anticipated correctly that my hands would be far too busy soothing distressed prickles to take the wheel. We were only half a mile or so from home, and as we drove, the little hedgehog possibly responding to the sudden warmth and the delights of Beethoven, stuck his head out of my jacket front, peered round curiously, and appeared quite content with his sudden change in fortune.

For those arriving at our house, the first impression must surely be the same. For some, it will indicate welcome and hospitality,

2

'Weighing the young Michael...'

while for others, one has to accept, it means noise, grubby paws, and cold noses proffered, sometimes in tactless places! In other words, dogs! We have four, three of whom are rescues, all much loved, inevitably vocal, and always delighted to see us come home. Suffice it to say that the night we arrived home with the latest addition, the greeting we got was well up to standard and joyously choral, while we attempted rather ineffectually to quell the riot, fearful lest we incur the wrath of slumbering and less canine-orientated neighbours at this nocturnal cacophony. Once inside the homely portals, each dog temporarily pacified with a hug and a choccy digestive, and settled in a basket, I was able to concentrate on a more thorough examination of the foundling. Ian, meanwhile, had pottered off to bed, happy to leave me in charge of matters erinacean .

My first job, now that I was sure he was uninjured, was to weigh the young hedgehog. This I did, without too much difficulty or irritation to the hedgehog, on my small kitchen scales, more often used for the weighing of cake ingredients and other such things. Placed firmly but gently in the plastic tray, he sat quite still, regarding me balefully, while I noted down his weight. On that night he weighed exactly seven ounces and I knew that, at that weight, he stood no chance at all of surviving the winter if left to his own devices. Over the years I had reared a number of young hedgehogs, and I realised that the next few weeks would be crucial if he were to survive.

In order to hibernate successfully, a young hedgehog should not be less than a pound in weight, and should have guzzled enough food to enable it to build up a good layer of fat to keep going over the long months of winter. For undernourished hedgehogs, the time of hibernation can be a time of danger,

4

and young hedgehogs are especially vulnerable if winter comes early and spring is late.

All being well, the average well-nourished and healthy hog will start turning its mind to building a nest round about early October, or even sooner if the weather is getting cold. A period of much business and activity ensues. Nesting material is collected in the mouth and carried to the chosen site. Dead leaves, hay, moss and perhaps old newspapers (one has a lovely picture of a hedgehog waking up in midwinter and sitting back with a copy of the Sun!) are all rounded up. The most likely sites for a good winter's kip are under garden sheds, in hay barns, beneath log-piles, deep under tree roots, etc; I even found the remains of a hibernacular, as these winter nests are called, inside an old bicycle basket at the back of our garage some years ago. Some sites, chosen for their apparent cosiness, may prove mortally dangerous to an unsuspecting hedgehog. Prospective bonfires, for instance, can be lethal for reasons we need not enlarge on, as can compost and manure piles. I dread to think how many blissfully dormant hogs have woken in the hedgehogs' Valhalla, having been roasted in a bonfire or impaled on a garden fork while curled up all unknowing in the warm depths of an aromatic dung heap. A great many hedgehogs would be spared an untimely demise with a little more foresight and vigilance on the part of us somewhat thick humans.

The average hibernacular is a veritable masterpiece of construction and design. Once the site is established and bedding rounded up, the hedgehog piles it all up, burrows into the centre and rotates, using its spines to sculpt and shape the lining of the nest. It is vital that the nest is waterproof, thickly lined and well insulated. In other words, a double-glazing salesman's dream! A new nest is built every year, though the same site

'We decided to call him Michael Heselspine...'

may well be used again with fresh 'duvet' and 'pillows' procured.

In a very mild winter, it is not unusual for hedgehogs to emerge from their nests and potter about looking for food, and they may even decide to construct a new nest on a different site. Hedgehogs seen out and about during cold spells, especially small ones, are probably feeling a bit 'crook' and should be examined for signs of injury or starvation.

Of course, the latest addition must have a name. I never consider any bird, beast or fish to be a true member of the family until it is christened, and it is nearly always those names that come to me in an inspirational flash that stick! Having recently, and somewhat to my horror, been roped in to help at the Conservative coffee morning, and with Michael Heseltine being much in the news at the time, I decided that, as an unashamed admirer of his general air of panache and fetching hair style, I would name our little hedgehog accordingly, and so it was that 'Michael Heselspine' became a member of our family!

Michael was quite unlike any hedgehog I had reared before, being endlessly friendly, curious, and amazingly unafraid of us humans or our other animals. Settled in a large rabbit hutch in the utility room, where he could hear *The Archers* on my portable radio in the kitchen and keep an eye on things generally, he had a warm sleeping area and enough space for exercise and pottering. Never did I have the feeling that he wanted to escape, unlike other hogs who had used us for B&B in the past, some of whom had gone nearly batty trying to escape, and had made the whole place feel rather like Colditz. He thrived from day one, and so rapidly became part of the household that it was hard to imagine life without him.

'Happy to sit in a small basket on the kitchen counter…'

'Passing the time of day with a china robin...'

'Michael the Christmas Hedgehog...'

9

Michael actually seemed to enjoy being handled, relaxing instantly when picked up, and poking his head out to peer round myopically. He seldom rolled up into the customary ball, and was perfectly happy to sit in a small basket on the kitchen counter observing me as I moved about organising the evening meal. Sleeping soundly by day, he usually began to stir and shuffle about at the sound of *The Archers'* signature tune, ambling round his pen sniffing the air and visiting his bowl for sips of water.

Weeks went by, and winter came in with a vengeance, bringing deep snow and icy winds for days on end. I shuddered to think what would have happened to Michael Heselspine if we had not happened upon him that night in October.

Michael ate voraciously, polishing off half a tin of dog food a day, and in the words of the Bible 'grew, and waxed strong'. Christmas came, with Michael emerging from his sleeping quarters in time to partake of a turkey wing with huge enthusiasm. Entering into the seasonable spirit, he posed most tastefully on a mock snow background, passing the time of day with a particularly lifelike china robin to have his photograph taken.

This was followed by a happy couple of hours trogging round the sitting room amidst the piles of discarded wrapping paper and cardboard boxes, and retiring to his nest only when he had polished off the shattered remains of a turkey drumstick and had had a bit of a go at a mince pie, round about midnight. My ten-year old daughter, Lucy, had suggested that a paper hat might be nice, but as they all seemed a little on the large size, we scrapped the idea.

To remove a wild creature from its natural habitat and introduce it to human domesticity is something that should never be undertaken lightly. I would never advocate enforcing captivity in any wild creature purely for the sake of it, but if a wild bird or animal is brought in sick or injured, then of course everything possible should be done to rescue, resuscitate and help that bird or animal recuperate before returning it to its natural state.

Over the years many such have passed through my hands and, in nearly every case, brightened and enriched our lives. One simply never knows what will turn up next. A knock at the door may herald a brace of children (they never come singly, always in pairs: safety in numbers, perhaps!), small hands clutching the maimed, the halt, the blind, or merely the unwanted and superfluous. Cardboard boxes containing bedraggled foundlings often appear on my doorstep, while phone calls from anxious acquaintances or, more likely, from total strangers, produce a succession of creatures to be cured or cosseted, and some, inevitably, buried.

There hardly seems to have been a time when I did not have some waif or stray under my roof: young rabbits, orphaned by sad mischance or by marauding Jack Russells; copious varieties of birds with broken wings, severed legs or gunshot wounds; the odd stray cat, and many more. The succession has been endless. I remember especially 'Captain Frobisher', the handsome herring gull found entangled in a fishing net leaving one leg limp and useless. The vet amputated, and after weeks of convalescence, the gallant captain was soon swimming happily up and down in our avocado bath, his remaining leg paddling away like fury. Supplied with pails of rather smelly fish scraps by our friendly local fish man, himself something of an amateur ornithologist, the debonair and spunky Frobisher did well, and was quite capable of coping by the time we returned him first to a manageable rock pool for a trial run, and then to the open sea, where we watched him paddle off, albeit slightly lopsidedly, to join a huddle of fellow gulls, who were doing a little quiet fishing some thirty feet from the beach.

Returning a bird or animal fit and well to its natural home always gives me a tremendous feeling of achievement and satisfaction along with some sadness at the parting. Inevitably, one has to accept occasional defeat and a sensation of having somehow failed as yet another small corpse is consigned to the earth.

Burying anything in our garden has become increasingly hazardous over the years. More recent funerals, usually conducted with appropriate solemnity by Lucy, decked in her Dad's rather shabby academic gown and my black furry hat, have been known to produce considerable consternation as it becomes clear that the chosen site is already occupied, while four dogs, all intent on a little clandestine archaeology, can cause mayhem in the graveyard. No area of our modest garden seems free of the corpses of hamsters, gerbils, mice, rabbits, guinea-pigs, goldfish, the odd rat, and probably not a few desiccated stick insets, all dear departed friends laid to rest in graves once marked with tiny wooden crosses or piles of pebbles, until a combination of time and the lawn mower cause markers to be destroyed.

The digging of flower beds and planting of new shrubs must needs be carefully planned and executed to avoid disturbing the quiet dead. Indeed, wails of anguish have been heard to come from Lucy at the sight of a long departed friend 'coming up the other way' during the most poignant moment of the latest funeral. But time heals, Lucy's grin returns, and 'could she please have an ardvaark for Xmas?!'

To wrap the deceased in a poly bag and smuggle it out to the bin men would of course be sacrilegious and quite unthinkable; meanwhile, such numerous interments undoubtedly cause problems for those of us who feel inspired to do a little gentle gardening. I know of no more unnerving sight than that of a mummified gerbil in an empty mayonnaise jar residing in the exact spot chosen for an expensive new dwarf conifer.

Having spent the first ten years of her life surrounded by animals, Lucy has had to learn to take the rough with the smooth. Funerals have become part and parcel of keeping pets, but certain things still produce instant and sometimes violent reaction. While she coped well on being woken in the middle of the night to discover, to her abject horror, that the entire contents of the stick insect tank had escaped and were marching en masse like a whole cohort of Roman soldiers up the wall and across the ceiling of her room, the sight of a bloated little wood-mouse floating bug-eyed and lifeless in a bucket of rain-water into which it had misguidedly dived, or the vision of dozens of writhing moths and flies crucified suicidally on the wet paint of our newly decorated sun-porch, cause her to lament inconsolably. I was just the same at her age when even the sight of a long dead wood-louse filled me with deep sorrow.

By mid-January, Michael Heselspine had gained eight ounces, was distinctly perky, and had his picture taken for the local paper sitting in a glass beer mug with a Tory rosette sellotaped to it. This blaze of publicity made him something of a local celebrity overnight. Rather unfortunately, I happened to be holding the beer mug at the time, and though Michael passed his screen test with flying colours, the overall result of a high-powered close-up lens on my crow's feet and double chin were distinctly less flattering, and, for a while, it was I who felt far more inclined to consider hibernation than 'megastar Michael'! In truth I know of nothing more twitch-making than appearing in the local rag with my rather middle-aged visage in glorious close-up, especially as the two of us had made the front page!

Publicity in the newspapers brings many and varied results. For Michael it brought fame and public adulation. For yours truly it brought endless leg-pulling and pig-sticking! 'When are you going to be promoted to page three!' was the usual rather inappropriate query, usually accompanied by a nod and a wink from chaps of my acquaintance. Alternatively, 'Close-ups can be so cruel, but they do say the camera never lies' from female friends (so-called)!

A more positive result of the newspaper article was that I received numerous phone calls from members of the newly-formed Michael Heselspine fan club, enquiring as to his well-being and health, and often seeking advice about their own and other people's hedgehog problems.

I suppose it was inevitable that I should become known as the 'Hedgehog Lady'. Actually, I think it's rather nice, and not altogether too terribly surprising for, as Lucy observes, were I to don a mob-cap and a pinny, I might very well pass for Mrs Tiggy-winkle in the dusk with the light behind me!

For several weeks after our appearance in print the phone was still ringing. People were desperate for advice on hedgehog husbandry; several noble souls even got into their cars, some driving many miles, to visit Michael, or, on several occasions, to bring me tiny hoglets. Such a lady was Irene, who drove all of thirty miles over hill and dale to bring a tiny waif. Sadly it died only hours after its arrival, but Irene and I have become friends and swop hedgehog notes over the phone regularly. Irene had three small hogs, all rescued in early winter, and all doing well. 'Come to coffee, and bring your Hedgehog' was the invitation over the phone one day, and thus it was that I was able to get some photos of Michael in close proximity with others of his kind, and the first faint stirrings of ideas for this little book began.

Chapter II

More of Me

At the age of five, and embarking on my early education, I was sent to a convent school called St Francis. There, I was instantly enchanted to discover that we were apparently to be taught by penguins. It was quite a while before I was persuaded that these smiling, chattering black and white figures were not penguins at all, but ladies dressed up in funny clothes pretending to be penguins! So unwilling was I to accept this unwelcome revelation, and as the ladies had obviously gone to tremendous trouble to look like penguins, entirely for our pleasure, of course, I would reward their efforts to please, and dub them 'Nunguins'.

At playtime, we would stampede to the toy-room. Here juice and biscuits were distributed, and we were allowed to play for half an hour, watched over by a smiling nunguin. My favourite toy was an exceedingly scruffy and dejected-looking brown felt rabbit with one-and-a-half ears, cross-eyes and numerous patches and darns. The other children never bothered with him, and so I went each playtime to gather him up and carry him to a corner for a spot of tender loving care. Then, one day, I was heartbroken to discover that my shabby little friend was no longer there. One of the nunguins, seeing the effect his disappearance was having on me, stepped in, clasped me to her starched white front and assured me gently and with supreme conviction that 'rabbit' had gone to live with kind St Francis and all the other good little bunnies, where he would be mended and have two proper ears again, and not be old or worn out any more. Never for one moment did it occur to me that the poor chap had in all likelihood gone head first into the convent dustbin!

My memories of the convent remain clear, even after all these years. Not only was I totally devoted to my nunguins, but I was fascinated by everything they did. They were forever fiddling with strings of beads that hung from their belts, and when not attending to us, appeared endlessly immersed in rather one-sided conversations with St Francis or, more exciting still, with something called a blessed virgin.

There were statues of Jesus all over the place, usually flashing a purple heart with prickles sticking out of it. This, coupled with the fact that most of the holy Jesuses also sported spiky hair bands filled me with some disquiet. Another vaguely worrying fact was that, in every one of the numerous paintings of Mary and baby Jesus, all the babies looked totally different, an observation that left me completely foxed.

Holy water was a source of tremendous interest to us five-year-olds. There was a little bowl of it on a stool outside the chapel door. The nunguins made us all dip the tips of two fingers into this and draw a cross on our foreheads. I seem to recall much speculation as to what would happen if one licked the wet fingers, or even snatched a quick swig from the bowl while the nunguins' backs were turned. It was generally reckoned that one would possibly be turned into a heavenly host, and soar at once to heaven, or, less appealingly, be sent hurtling downwards for interrogation at the hands of Satan in his snake-and-bat-infested kingdom.

After due consideration, I decided that to tamper with holy water was not altogether wise as I neither felt too happy about

18

flying solo anywhere, heaven or not, nor reckoned myself to be sufficiently keen on satanic wildlife to risk a trip downwards. Frogs and toads I could have coped with, being quite partial especially to the former, but the possibility of devilish spiders deterred me from further speculation.

Life at St Francis seemed to be one long Nativity Play. We were forever dressing up as angels, shepherds and kings following tin-foil stars, bearing gifts of tinsel-covered Malteser boxes, or watching over a rather moth-eaten flock of cardboard sheep by night. I loved every moment. The first year I was Mary in one of nanny's blue nighties. The next year I topped the bill in feathery wings and glittery wire halo as the angel Gabriel, and, despite my wings' starting to moult in the first scene, quite definitely stole the show! The third year was something of an anticlimax, as I found myself relegated to the ranks of lowly shepherds, with a Woolie's tea towel on my head, held firmly in place by a bit of old pyjama cord.

By the time I left the convent I had made up my mind that St Francis was a thoroughly good bloke, altogether a chap to look up to and admire. In every picture I saw of him, he was surrounded by tranquil-looking rodents of various shapes and sizes, and invariably had a selection of adoring birds perched all over him. Looking back, I think that my association with the good St Francis almost certainly marked the first stirrings of my love of animals, in particular, those unfortunate or unloved.

When I was ten, I decided to be a ballerina. To float across the stage as a dying swan in front of a packed and spellbound audience became my sole desire, though I do recall at the time being somewhat concerned as to the welfare of the apparently ailing swan.

By now at a small school in Kent, I revelled in the dance and drama lessons and itched to perform on the grassy tree-flanked stage which lent itself so wonderfully to outdoor productions.

We were to do 'A Midsummer Night's Dream' and I, who longed to be the one in the ass's head, was, to my mortification, cast as a toadstool. How well I remember the sheer frustration I felt at being told that under no circumstances whatsoever was I to move an inch, let alone dance. I simply had to stand throughout the whole performance looking inscrutable and fungus-like right at the back of the stage. The sensations of thwarted ambition and wasted talent were unimaginable, made worse by the fact that my *bête noire* from the lower III was cast as Puck. She was slim, pretty and very talented, and I hated her. Perfect as Puck, she leapt and skipped around the stage, pausing now and then to prod me with a green-painted finger and put out her tongue. Half-way through the second act there was a torrential downpour which left me rooted to the spot wrapped like an Egyptian mummy in swathes of sodden crêpe paper, my once impressive toadstool top all droopy like a down-at-the-heel Ascot hat. My only consolation was that Puck proceeded to get her 'come-uppance' by skidding on the rain-drenched grass and falling flat on her beastly face.

My next appearance on the outdoor stage the following summer term proved every bit as disastrous as the doomed toadstool. I was evicted unceremoniously from the feathered ranks of the 'Eleven Swan Princes' at the dress rehearsal, when the old harridan who passed as our headmistress halted proceedings and pointed out that, as I was noticeably more substantial than the other ten swan princes, the chorus was lopsided and top-heavy. Thus, I was banished to the ranks of earthy peasants where I sulked as a hessian-draped hag, and hated every moment.

'Visiting Hammy in his cage...'

Despite this seemingly endless succession of theatrical put-downs, I persevered, remaining determined to follow the up-hill pathway to stardom. I continued to turn up for all play and panto auditions, despite being dubbed either the 'sugar pig' fairy or the 'sugar plump' fairy by my less charitable but far lighter-of-foot class-mates.

Ballet lessons in the village hall brought forth a variety of would-be Giselles and Sleeping Beauties. Those of us who had nannies brought them along. The nannies sat around the sides of the hall in their squashy felt hats and sensible shoes, chatting discreetly among themselves and beaming fondly as each of their own particular charges pirouetted by, or succeeded in executing a passable *grand jeté* without actually falling flat on her face.

Then, one day, the final axe fell, and the world of ballet was robbed once and for all of a future star. Our teacher, herself a retired ballerina of some renown, stick-thin and as unsmiling as a papier-mâché gargoyle, eyed me stonily and ordered the lady at the piano to stop playing. You could have heard a pin drop, even the nannies were rigid with apprehension. Pointing a bony finger at me, and in sepulchral tones, she observed that I appeared to have at least six inches of green winceyette knickers showing, and would I kindly pull them up immediately, as no true ballerina would be seen dead sporting such items of underwear. To a dumpy self-conscious little girl this was the ultimate shame and degradation. Amidst the titters of my fellow dancers and the sympathetic headshakes of the nannies, especially my own, I fled, yanking up the accursed bloomers as I went, and never danced again.

The last experience affected me perhaps more than I realised at the time. I withdrew into myself and spent more and more time with my animals and drawing horses.

Nanny was a splendid ally during those years. She was of the old school of nannies who simply don't exist any more, and would still ask if we had hankies and had we remembered to say 'thank you' long after we were all grown up. She had come as a temporary for one of my brothers, and was only taken on for five weeks. In the end she stayed nearly fifty years, seeing us all grow up, and staying on with the family to administer cod-liver oil and smacked bottoms to the next generation. Over my teenage years, she was my special friend and confidante, helping to clean out hutches, nurse sick creatures and even to wield a hammer while helping turn the garden shed into a loose-box for my first pony. How bravely she took my part after I'd waved back cheerfully at an auctioneer at our local market, and found myself the ecstatic owner of a small white goat! Needless to say, the goat was not permitted and was returned to the rather baffled auctioneer, but it was nanny who said that I had shown initiative and enterprise while all about me scolded and forbade further visits to the market.

In those days dances were held in private houses or the golf club etc. Discos had not been invented, thank God, for I doubt I would have been able to stand the ghastly din and flashing lights. Even so, I started off at a disadvantage in that I was not in the least partial to boys who, in their turn, most certainly did not fancy me. Inevitably, I found myself a wallflower and was usually thankful to be so.
My own special way of coping with dances was first to locate the food, load up my plate with all the most fattening goodies, then go and sit on the stairs or in the loo with the family dog or cat. Indeed, one of the more enjoyable dances I ever went to

was spent curled up in a large dog basket with half a chocolate cake, three Jack Russells and a bantam, watching an episode of Rawhide on the cook's black and white telly.

When I was thirteen, I was interned deep in the Kent countryside at a girl's boarding school. Life seemed dull indeed, and I missed the company of my many pets left at home under the beady eye of nanny and the kindly gardener.

I hated all games, especially those that required genuine exertion such as running. Hockey and lacrosse were my biggest trials, and when it was discovered that I filled up almost the entire goal when clad in two sets of body-guards, I was made goalkeeper for all practice games and matches. Under normal circumstances, I would not have been considered for any team in a million years, but my vast, hugely padded figure in goal somehow managed to instil some hint of wariness among opposing teams. And so I seemed doomed to stand for long hours on freezing afternoons like a dejected Michelin man, while my more athletic contemporaries thundered up and down the pitch yelling like Indians on the war path, loving every minute, and slugging lightning-quick balls in my direction, most of which shot past me to jubilant shrieks of 'GOAL'!!

The physical demands of the gymnasium held equal horrors. I simply was not designed to excel in any form of athletic activity. Even swimming, which I rather liked, brought underhand insinuations appertaining to beached whales etc. from the games mistress, who, of course, should have known better.
Then, one day, I was summoned to the headmistress's study. Off I trotted, hoping that, with any luck, the school governors had finally decided I was a hopeless case, and, so as not to jeopardise the honour of the school any more than was

'Guinea-Pig meets Hedge Pig!'

absolutely necessary, had decided to play safe and expel me. Not so; the headmistress, who was getting on in years and rather arthritic, asked me if I would perhaps consider becoming her regular dog walker. The endearing old soul requested me most earnestly to think hard as it would, of course, mean that I should have to give up all games henceforth. I could not believe my good luck! And so it was that for my last eighteen months in the school, I'd set out each afternoon with a spiky bow-legged mongrel called Towser on one side, and a somewhat overweight but affable black labrador called Chris on the other. Together we roamed the fields and woods that surrounded the school, and no one could have been happier than I with my new role as custodian of the school dogs.

At seventeen I had to accept that my latest ambition, to be a vet, like many another before it, was not to be realised, for how can one hope to become a vet with two 'O'levels to one's name, especially when the two in question happen to be scripture and drawing! And so I left the school with only two accolades to speak of, apart from clocking up a considerable mileage with the school dogs. One of these was that, as far as the old bag of a games mistress knew, I had never once, in the five years I'd been in the school, actually succeeded in landing on the far side of the vaulting horse, while the other, more on the academic side, was that I had once managed to achieve 2% for a maths exam when in the lower IV. I was informed somewhat icily that one of these marks was for neatness and the other for spelling my name correctly!

My rather unusual name still produces the odd jibe about King Arthur and magicians, etc. but in fact, it has stood me in quite good stead in that it is not a name that people forget, which if you are a struggling artist or would-be writer can be an advantage. I had a lot of teasing about it at school, though I, for one, was endlessly thankful that I wasn't yet another Charlotte, Camilla or Alexandra or, worse still, Penelope, which I gather I very nearly was. In this age of untold droves of Traceys, Kylies, Sharons and Michelles, it is, I have to say, rather nice to be a little different. Inevitably I get the odd variation. Marleen and Mervin I can just about cope with, but do rather draw the line at Myrtle!

So ended my school days, and it was with an unexpected sense of sadness tinged with distinct relief that I threw my school panama hat out of the train window as we rolled across a bridge over the Thames en route for the traditional slap-up tea in Harrods. The next day, we all left the school for ever and went out into the world.

When I was twenty-one, my father asked me if I would like to have a 'coming out' dance. My elder sister had been presented at court and gone on to do something rather mysterious called 'the season'. On observing my form in a full-length mirror, however, I came to the conclusion that I was quite far enough 'out' already; and as local 'debs' delights' of my acquaintance were, to a man, totally devoid of either chins or character, I opted instead for an archaeological jaunt round Greece as a twenty-first birthday present.

Mercifully, being presented at court was by that time defunct, which was probably just as well, as I would almost certainly have blotted my copy-book by chatting up the royal corgis when I should have been curtseying to their royal owner.

Attempting to enter into the country way of life I did, at this time, try a little basic hunting, shooting and fishing. I have to say that all three pastimes were, for me at any rate, an unmitigated disaster. I hunted only once and was ordered home after just half an hour for overtaking the master at about eighty miles an hour. Fishing was hopeless. I simply couldn't cope with the way the fish's eye fixed on me as I removed the hook. Shooting was even worse. The only time I went out with a gun, I shot a hare. It screeched for twenty minutes before expiring, and yours truly spent the rest of the day under sedation in a darkened room.

While I would never attempt to press my views on others who do enjoy such pastimes, I have to admit they are not for me. Living in an area where all these 'sports' thrive, I hold my peace. Yet I simply cannot equate the word 'sport' with having to practically hurl the ridiculously tame local pheasants into the air in order to get them sufficiently airborne for the waiting guns.

My next step up the ladder of life was art school, from whence I was quite quickly ejected for the persistent and disruptive drawing of horses all over every available flat surface, including walls.

Life drawing absolutely revolted me. It never failed to amaze me how the sight of overblown naked ladies, most of whom smoked cigars and more closely resembled baskets of melons than women, could reduce my male contemporaries to heaps of gibbering fascination, while the sight of a scrawny man clad only in rather grubby and inadequate 'fig leaves' held no enchantment for me at all. One of our regular models was a young and singularly unattractive Quentin Crisp, whose mauve hair, green eye shadow and vivid lipstick made me all the more convinced that I definitely preferred drawing animals to humans.

As any life-drawing that I did manage to complete appeared distinctly equine in form, a fact which did little for my standing with the teachers, I decided that, in future, I would concentrate on horse portraits.

From art school I went and looked after a herd of pedigree dairy goats in Sussex. The herd was owned by a wonderful goat lady called Liz Dove. I stayed for a year, and it was from Liz that I learnt so much, not only about the care of animals, but how they think and act and, above all, how wonderfully funny they can be.

I'm sure that anyone who keeps goats would agree that there is never a dull moment. Goats are such characters, and are highly intelligent. Liz kept several different varieties. There were some of the pure white Saanans, a few pretty coffee-and-cream Toggenburgs and a fair smattering of odd-coloured 'mongrels', mostly rescues. Our main milk producers were the handsome and many-coloured Anglo-Nubians with their aristocratic Roman noses and long floppy ears.

Apart from the usual chores connected with goat husbandry, like cleaning out, grooming and feeding, the actual milking took up considerable time. Much as I loved the goats, I did find hauling myself out of bed at 6.30 on a wintry morning somewhat daunting, though the inside of the goat shed was lovely and warm and smelled wonderfully of sleepy goats and hay. Each nanny was tucked up in her own little pen, with the chaps in another shed across the yard. As soon as I opened the shed door in the morning I'd be greeted by a positive cacophony of welcoming bleats, and I would start off by going into each pen to greet the occupant with a big hug and a gentle ear pull.

One of my more exacting jobs was to accompany the pedigree

goats to the many shows held over the summer. At the dairy show in London we stayed overnight, and I would bed down, curled in a sleeping-bag to keep watch over my valuable charges. Determined pot-hunting dog or horse ladies are bad enough when it comes to outshining the opposition in the ring, but, believe me, goat women take a bit of beating. The more manic among them are formidable in the extreme and, with some, one cannot rule out the possibility of actual sabotage. The surreptitious squirting of a rival's udder with gentian violet, thus rendering it vivid purple and therefore unlikely to impress the judge, is one thing, and it could even have its amusing side, but to feed another goat poison greens, such as yew, is about as low as one can stoop. Sadly these and other forms of sabotage were not unknown among the show-goat fraternity. Mercifully we had no trouble, as I remember, but be assured that I was ready to defend my pedigree charges with every drop of my blood, had a dastardly goat-nobbler put in an appearance.

I remember one quite amusing incident that happened while I was with the goats. Liz had rescued a little scrub goat from an uncaring local farmer. She had arrived sad, very thin and covered in lice. Three months later she was a different lady, though not necessarily a reformed character. Christened Ethel, she ruled the herd and us with a hoof of iron. How well I remember the sight of the fully recovered and exceedingly mischievous Ethel standing on her hind legs with an expression of rapt concentration on her face, chipping away meticulously with a razor sharp front hoof at the black and gold lettering on Liz's new van on which, at great expense, a local signwriter had inscribed the name of the herd.

Another memory of Walnut Tree Farm that remains especially etched in my mind is a remarkable, if sad one. Liz had a large yellow and blue macaw called Mac who, while he was particularly devoted to Liz's husband Graham, had taken an instant dislike to me the day I had arrived. He possessed not only the beadiest of eyes that missed nothing, but also a beak that was capable of cracking a walnut with both speed and ease. As he was not above a little practice on a carelessly proffered finger, I steered clear, giving my undivided attention and affection to the other animals which ranged from piglets, dogs, cats and assorted poultry, not to mention the goats.

One night towards the end of my stay with Liz and Graham, I was sitting up in bed with a copy of the *Horse and Hound*, when I heard a scratching sound. The cats and dachshunds were all, to my knowledge, asleep in the kitchen with the door shut, and Liz and Graham were out, so not unnaturally, I became a trifle apprehensive, especially as the sound was quite definitely coming nearer.

Instead of a door, I had a heavy velvet curtain which, on this occasion, was drawn across the entrance of my room. Sitting up in bed, by now thoroughly alarmed, I was horrified to see the bottom of the curtain start to move. By now scared stiff, I sat bolt upright in bed and waited with bated breath. After further scratchings and twitchings of the curtain, I was amazed to see Mac's blue and yellow head appear round the bottom of the curtain. Pausing for a moment, he shuffled into the room, across the floor and, to my horror, began to climb up the bed clothes on to the bed. By now I realised that something must surely be very wrong, and that I almost certainly had nothing to fear.

Sitting quite still, I talked to him, using the little clucking noises I knew he liked to hear. Laboriously he waddled up the bed and gently poked his head under my arm, settling quietly into the eiderdown across my lap. He stayed there for an hour, hardly moving at all, pressed against me and occasionally emitting

'Looking picturesque in a floral setting ...'

subdued peeping noises as I stroked his head. It was thus that Liz found us when she came home and, summoned by a call from me, looked round the curtains.

By mid-morning the following day poor Mac was dead, having suffered a massive haemorrhage later that night. He must have known that he was ill and had probably been in considerable pain. Sensing that Liz and Graham were not there to help him, he had left his stand in the sitting room and come to find me. The vet did a post mortem later that day and found that Mac was suffering from the later stages of cirrhosis of the liver, and could not have been helped even if it had been diagnosed much earlier. We were all shocked and saddened, and even I, who had never taken to him, have not ceased to wonder at, and appreciate, the trust he showed in me when in deep distress.

When I left Liz and the goats, I got a job as a vet's assistant in Herne Bay. It lasted three months, was something of a disaster, and made me realise that, even if I had been bright enough to have qualified as a vet, I would have been quite hopeless. I found it hard enough to cope with the endless succession of sick and injured animals, but simply could not come to terms with the tragic numbers of healthy dogs, cats, rabbits etc. brought into our surgery to be put down by people whose only excuse seemed to be that they no longer had the time or inclination to look after them.

In the 1960s, animal rescue centres were nothing like as thick on the ground as they are now, and the vets, however unwilling, were more or less obliged to euthanase and dispose of any animal that had become unwanted.

The operating theatre fascinated me, despite my apparent

allergy to ether and the smell of chemicals. I'd watch entranced while my skilful employer, who was at his best with small animals, mended shattered bones, removed obstructions and repaired the often horrendous results of road accidents. We treated just about everything from anaemic tortoises to Pekineses with toothache. Several hedgehogs came our way, as I remember, as did a distinctly bolshy badger who had cut himself badly on broken glass.

The crunch came one day as my boss set-to to deliver a litter of miniature dachshund puppies by Caesarean. I watched with interest as the unconscious little bitch was rolled onto her back and strapped into place with her bulging tummy, tight as a drum, exposed ready for the scalpel. The first puppy to be delivered was huge, had one eye in the middle of its forehead, was hopelessly deformed, and appeared to be dead. Quickly laying the grotesque thing on a side table, I turned once more to the recumbent dachshund, ready to receive the next pup. It was only when I turned back to the side table again, this time armed with a wriggling healthy chipolata-like pup, that I saw to my absolute horror that the hideous one-eyed thing, not dead at all, was stirring, uttering wheezy snuffling sounds, and trying to crawl across the tabletop. I just about managed to put the squeaking puppy down safely before I conked out and spent the rest of the Caesarean flat on my back on the surgery floor.

My understanding vet and I parted company with regret on my side and, I suspect, not a little relief on his. Apart from my apparent inability to remain conscious during operations, I suspect that my performance in the actual field had not entirely impressed. There was no doubt that I was not altogether at my athletic best when required to corner a full-grown Aberdeen Angus bull with a view to inserting eye drops, let alone trying to persuade a muscular and very randy colt that castration was no more than a mere pin-prick. Gerbils with bald tails and guinea- pigs with vertigo were rather more my scene, but as a paid veterinary assistant, I was, quite rightly, expected to be a useful all-rounder. I'd learnt a lot from my vet during the months I was with him, and regretted not a minute, but finally had to admit that the veterinary life was not for me.

When I had recovered from my short stint of animal nursing, I decided that it was high time that I saw a bit of the world, so I went to America. I had always longed to be a cowboy, or, in my case, by now, a considerably-less-tubby-than-of-old cowgirl. I was very lucky, and walked into a job on a cattle ranch on the Montana/Wyoming border. Here I proceeded to exist in complete bliss for the next six months.

I was the ranch cook. This, in a nutshell, entailed coming up with breakfast for ten ranch hands at 6.30 am, doing as I chose all day, then producing a huge meal for the boys again at suppertime. My domain was a large log cabin, complete with stuffed buffalo's head over the fireplace, and a built-in pack-rat colony under the floorboards. It was here that I ate, slept, cooked, and generally reigned supreme.

The boys I cooked for decided from day one that, apart from being plum crazy and a real 'dude', I was, on the whole, pretty harmless. They tolerated my efforts to cook steak, and a strange substance called hominy grits, not to mention eggs and pancakes for breakfast, and even condescended to smack their lips and compliment my chocolate cake and flapjacks at supper.

It was heaven to have most of each day to myself. My boss had turned a shade of green when I announced that I'd like to ride cowboy-style while I was there. Thinking, I suppose, to cure me of such madness, he pointed me in the direction of a corral, where a dozen or so horses of various size and colour were dozing, and announced that, if I could get near enough to any of them to put a saddle on it, I could ride. This proved rather more of a challenge than I'd anticipated. The ranch-bred Quartre horses were used to being roped and caught-up by expert cowhands, and did not take too kindly to being pursued round the corral by a 'greenhorn' from England waving a carrot. However, numerous carrots and considerable patience eventually prevailed, and after many misses, I finally succeeded in cornering a little liver chestnut mare, who, I suspect, more out of a mixture of curiosity and amazement, eventually allowed me to put a bridle and saddle on her. The mare's name was Sanka, and it is to her that I owe the wonderfully happy memories of being a 'real' cowgirl in the American west.

My morning chores done, I'd lure Sanka into a corner of the corral, carrot in hand, saddle up and ride for hours. I rode in a genuine western saddle and bridle, wore leather breeches, cowboy boots, and sported a very natty felt stetson. The boys found the delight I took in my cowboy image quite hilarious and christened me 'Calamity Jane'.

However, they must have had some faith in my prowess in the saddle, as they allowed me to ride with them on an all-day cattle round-up and took me along to the local rodeo where I saw bucking broncos, barrel racing, roping contests and brahmin bull riding. It was all quite splendid, and an experience I'll never forget.

The country round the ranch was magic. One paddock alone might stretch for ten miles, the land so bright and varied, rocky outcrops of vivid pink sandstone rising from rolling plainland of ochre and green sage-bush. It was just as I had imagined it, and exactly the backdrop to every cowboy film I'd ever seen.

The ranchland bordered on that of an Indian reservation. The whole area had once been the home of the Cheyenne tribe, and I often met up with the now rather pitiful remains of this once proud tribe of Plains Indians on my rides. Sometimes, I'd ride Sanka to the Indian agency office and watch while members of the Cheyenne community queued for their weekly allowance of cash. This usually led to noisy but reasonably harmless drinking binges for the men, and much concentrated tobacco-chewing and raucous laughter for the women.

The American Indian has always fascinated me. I never miss a western on telly or at the cinema, and frequently get hissed at for cheering on the Indians or muttering audible expletives at the sight of John Wayne or Clint Eastwood banging away at some poor benighted red man with a death-dealing Colt revolver or Winchester rifle. It was easy to imagine the Cheyenne in their old way of life before the white men came, bringing disease and alcohol, and eventually wiping out the huge herds of buffalo upon whom the Cheyenne relied completely for their very existence.

I went one day to the battlefield on the Little Big Horn where combined tribes of Plains Indians had finally got the better of a certain George Armstrong Custer, and was forced to reflect that, all things considered, the cocky fellow got his just deserts. I found it highly satisfactory that, according to legend, one of the very few survivors of that notorious fracas was a horse.

Perhaps it goes without saying that it was the native animals of

Montana and Wyoming which made the greatest impression on me. Apart from the horses which were everywhere in large numbers, I regularly encountered the friendly neighbourhood skunk, a comic but rather unpredictable chap, in no way to be trifled with on account of skunk emissions being unbelievably nauseating and of a lingering nature. There was Charley the pack-rat who would peer down at me beadily from between the dusty horns of the stuffed buffalo head where he had a nest, and the ranch cat, an elderly rather morose feline with one ear missing, who'd rather have died than expend sufficient energy to sort out a passing pack-rat, and who existed purely to eat and sleep.

On my rides, I saw quite a variety of wildlife. Mule deer, jack-rabbits, porcupines, bobcats and the gloriously furry and endearing raccoons of Davy Crockett hat fame. I never needed my binoculars, for as long as I was on a horse, the wild animals were not at all afraid of me, and allowed Sanka to come quite near. At night the sound of huge Pavarotti-sized bullfrogs vied with symphonies of crickets, the baleful hoots of owls and the eerie call of the timid dog-like little coyote. The night-time was especially magical, and I'd never seen the moon so huge and silver before.

The only blight on my idyllic life at the ranch was that there was, believe it or not, no loo in my cabin!! This necessitated much to-ing and fro-ing to the main ranchhouse where they had all the 'mod cons'. I gathered that the ranch usually employed male cooks, in which case I suppose a built-in loo was somewhat less of a requirement. One has to admit that nocturnal calls of nature are coped with rather more easily by a chap. Being a true 'lady' born and bred, the idea of squatting bare-rumped in the sage-brush beneath a vast Montana moon held

'Michael Heselspine aged seven months...'

few attractions. One can only imagine the degree of disconcertion caused by the muffled but unmistakable gyrations of an irate rattlesnake whose nocturnal territory one has inadvertently invaded while answering the call of nature at 2.0 am. To be caught thus in extremely close proximity to a three-foot rattlesnake with the nearest doctor 90 miles away by helicopter was an experience never to be forgotten either by me, or, I suspect, the unfortunate reptile. On the one occasion that an encounter of this gravity did occur, I was lucky. The horrified snake took one look and vamoosed.

When the time came for me to leave the ranch, I felt more sad than I could have imagined. The place, the people and the animals were all magical, and I never cease to thank my lucky stars that I'd had a chance to go there. I left early one morning in the battered old pick-up, driven by one of the boys who had somehow managed to survive my cooking. They had all turned out to see me off for the Greyhound bus depot some fifty miles away. My last impression of the ranch was of little Sanka's chestnut face with its crooked blaze looking over the corral fence saying her own goodbye, and, I would like to think, wishing I were not going.

The next eighteen months were spent as a house matron at Fettes College in Edinburgh. The necessary qualifications for looking after little prep-school-age boys are basic, as I had discovered while working in several prep schools over the years. A firm hand, a good eye and a sense of humour are really all that most headmasters require. If you can also trot out some sort of first-aid certificate as well, so much the better. At least you have probably learnt how to cope with bloody noses, constipation, the effects of too much tuck, or sudden headaches brought on by the thought of an impending Latin exam. With teenage boys, like those I had under my wing at Fettes, it is rather a different kettle of fish. To start with, you do not show your nose in the shower room while the chaps are starkers. Seventeen-year-olds are blessed with anatomical naughties that are most certainly not for matronic eyes, and they are desperately self-conscious. I encountered quite a different range of problems than those I'd had to deal with in small prep schools. On the whole I prefer the smaller boys. They are so chirpy and, unlike girls of the same age, tend not to sulk or bear grudges on being ticked off or told to go and wash behind their ears for the umpteenth time. For a small consideration, i.e. a tube of Smarties or turn round the drive on matron's moped, small boys can often be persuaded to skip games, albeit at the risk of irritating the games master, in order to clean out matron's guinea-pig or bath matron's Jack Russell. The older boys were, on the whole, dears, and treated me rather like a tiresome big sister. The great advantage was that, as they were nearly all at least a foot taller than I, there was little use in my entering into any form of argument, and it was far less effort to demur and go along with things.

At prep school, you clean up after the little darlings, usually in your British Home Stores dressing gown at three in the morning, after an illegal midnight feast; darn socks; comfort the homesick; and mutter darkly about mothers who are too busy going to Wimbledon or Ascot to sew on little Crispin's name-tapes. You commiserate with little chaps whose mothers turn up on sports day clad in leopard-skin jump suits, you confiscate unsuitable tuck, and cope with crops of verrucas, small boys with smoker's coughs and endless bangs and bruises. With large boys, you have to be adept at counselling the lovelorn, ready to vet study walls for any girlie pictures unsuitable for the eyes of anyone's granny or the housemaster's wife, and be

41

prepared to carry out low-key searches for the odd bottle of forbidden booze. At the end of my time in the school I left a little older and considerably wiser, armed with a plastic bag containing a Fettes Rugger shirt and a large box of rather stale Newberry Fruits from the House Tutor, who had taken a bit of a shine to me.

Three weeks later I flew to Australia, where I worked for the next fourteen months doing very much the same as I'd done in America. I travelled round doing the odd job here and there, loving the people, the country and, needless to say, the animals. The wildlife of Australia is so varied and quite unbelievably prolific. To see wallabies, kangaroos, emus and koalas, all in their natural habitat, was out of this world.

I stayed mostly on sheep stations in N.S.W. and Queensland, turning my hand to just about anything, including a bit of shearing, much to the fascination of the shearing gang, who had never before come across a female daft enough to want to do it. I lost one job very smartly. The fat, beer-swilling farmer who gave me a couple of weeks' work in exchange for food and a bunk, had a lot of trouble on his land with wombats who took great delight in digging up his paddocks in the silent watches of the night, thus creating havoc. Determined to put a stop to this, the furious farmer dashed round setting particularly nasty traps into which the unsuspecting wombats would go and then find themselves unhurt, but unable to escape. The brute would then ride round the traps early in the morning and shoot dead any wombat unfortunate enough to have got itself caught. Unable to stand the thought of this, I'd get up even earlier and rush round the traps, liberating as many wombats as I could. Sadly, both for me and the wombats, the horrid chap cottoned on to this and caught me red-handed one morning. I was at once dubbed 'a bloody Pommie Sheila' by the fat boozy farmer and his equally unprepossessing wife, who had, if I remember rightly, a face not unlike a haddock having difficulty spawning. After this I fled, guilt-ridden at having abandoned the wombats, and went to work with horses.

In Sydney, I got a job 'strapping' or grooming at the yearling sales. This led to a job with the N.S.W. Polo team exercising polo ponies. It was wonderful, but perhaps a trifle too energetic for me as the ponies were all terribly full of beans, not to mention oats, went flat out most of the time, and had me off with alarming regularity.

Despite the heat and a definite tendency towards vertigo, I climbed Ayers Rock clad in my Fettes rugger shirt, and apart from what might have been a disastrous encounter with a very venomous-looking spider on a loo-seat in the camp site at Alice Springs, had a wonderful time, and was very sad indeed when my work permit expired and I had to fly home.

The blissful estate of matrimony managed to elude me until I was thirty-nine, knocking on forty. Ian was forty-one and it was first time round for both of us. We were what the vicar who married us tactfully described as a 'slightly more mature couple'. No one was more amazed about the whole thing than I was, as I had long since resigned myself to being 'on the shelf' and had opted quite cheerfully for being eccentric, single, and an enthusiastic breeder of guinea-pigs and gerbils.

There had certainly been the odd chap over the years, but somehow they all managed to side-step any sort of long term commitment, having, I had good reason to believe, spotted the almost certain drawbacks to a lifelong liaison with yours truly. I

43

have to admit that it takes a special sort of man to put up with and be genial to the endless assortment of creatures who they could not have failed to notice shared my life.

Ian was something of a novice, having never, as I discovered early on in our courtship, actually owned any sort of pet in his life. He was intrigued, perhaps a trifle mystified, but seemingly not to be put off; I, sensing the long-term possibilities, set about indoctrinating him gently, but firmly, into the fascinations of rodent-rearing, hedgehog husbandry, and most important of all, the hitherto undiscovered delights of Jack Russell ownership.

When we finally decided to tie the knot, my father welcomed his prospective son-in-law with open arms. Not only had some stoic fellow finally agreed to relieve him of his spinster daughter, but this brave gentleman was, he discovered, as ardent a steam train buff as he was himself, and therefore well up to the mark and infinitely suitable.

As for me, I couldn't have netted a better soul mate. He is endlessly patient and long-suffering, not just where the animals are concerned, but also with my never-ending and somewhat wan efforts to stick with yet another miracle diet, be a good and thrifty housewife, and generally fill the marital bill. Very few things get him really riled, though I have seen the odd flash of temperament over minor set-backs, such as catching me doling out his favourite and very expensive muesli to the gerbils, or the time I surreptitiously commandeered two pairs of his well-loved but exceedingly elderly Y-fronts as dusters, in the firm belief that, owing to the lattice-work effect in unfortunate places, it was more than high time that they were pensioned off.

Motherhood, coming upon me as it did at the ripe old age of

nearly forty-two, was something of a shock, owing to the fact that, because of some fairly major tummy problems in my twenties, I had been warned that kiddywinks were a distinct unlikelihood. This piece of medical information had never bothered me as I'd always infinitely preferred baby animals to baby humans anyhow, and had been for years more than content with Jack Russells.

It was some weeks before I was able to come to terms with impending motherhood. The mere fact that the revolting little 'do-it-yourself' pregnancy testing kit purchased discreetly for me by a chum at our local chemist had, to my utter amazement, proved positive, left me shattered. Ian, needless to say, was absolutely over the moon. All of a dither, I fled to my GP squawking that I simply couldn't for the life of me think how on earth it could have happened. His somewhat predictable response to all this was that it was quite the best news he'd had that week, and that if I didn't know how it had happened by now, I never would, and made me an appointment for the next baby clinic at our local hospital.

My first visit to the hospital caused something of a stir when the head of the baby department, a very eminent man in his field, on being informed of my advanced age and the fact that not only had I had twin great aunts, twin second cousins, and was myself a twin, turned a shade pale, deserted his Christmas glass of sherry with matron and staggered down the corridor to view me for himself. A scan was arranged for later that month, and this confirmed, much to the relief of all concerned, especially the medical staff, a single exceedingly healthy and active embryo which was, to my great joy, a female of the species. Thus, I settled back into a blissfully trouble-free, though somewhat bovine pregnancy. For some light relief, I joined our local panto group and became, I believe, the only recorded specimen of a pregnant demon king. Clad fetchingly in red tights and an all-enveloping cloak, I lumbered demoniacally around the stage waving a lethal-looking toasting-fork while sporting spangly carrots on my head to look like horns.

Lucy overshot her arrival date by ten days and was eventually delivered yelling her head off in the middle of one of the most oppressive heat waves for years. Weighing in at nearly ten pounds, with a shock of black hair and a button nose, she leant more towards the bull-terrier rather than the Jack Russell, and from day one commenced to rule us with a small pink paw of iron. I, meanwhile, realising that my life had changed for ever, a fact which I accepted with huge pleasure and the anticipation of fun to come, lay back in my hospital bed, cocked a mental snook at those who had told me I'd probably never be a mum and blessed those responsible for inventing Caesarean sections!

I have to say that, though Lucy started life resembling a small bull-terrier, she is, as I write this ten years after her birth, now rather more akin to a saluki or a lean and athletic whippet, having wisely elected to take after dad in build. In that she showed an early affinity with all things furred and feathered, I noted with pleasure that she also had a good streak of mum in her as well. She tends to be a thinker rather than a doer, constantly pondering on matters weighty such as, how would the Queen react should MP David Blunkett's guide dog need to pee in the middle of the state opening of parliament; or who is caring for the stray dogs and cats of Sarajevo; and is poor Prince Charles still sad about his lost Jack Russell?

Being a much older mum inevitably produces the odd challenge. I am regularly mistaken for 'Gran', an error which elicits gales of mirth from Lucy! Requests for a frogspawn hunting expedition just as one is about to put up one's trotters in front of *Neighbours* at the end of a long day, or the daunting prospect of the mothers' race on sports day are, to say the least, somewhat nerve-racking when you're rising fifty-three. I have to remind myself that I am doing with Lucy things that most ladies of my age are doing with their grandchildren! Rest assured, however, I wouldn't have it any other way.

Chapter III

Back To Matters Prickly

But enough of me. It was spring, and in the normal course of events, Michael should have been returning to the wild. By late April the weather was getting warmer, and Michael was fat and engagingly active. By now, resident in a spacious pen in a grassy corner of the garden, he gave every sign of being both extremely content and glowingly healthy. Emerging from his box at dusk, he'd set off round the pen at a jog, snuffling and grunting. As soon as his food bowl appeared, he'd pounce, chomping and slurping with obvious enjoyment, emitting sounds not at all unlike a gum-chewing American.

I realised that decision time had come. Was Michael Heselspine to risk his neck in the great wide world, or was he to stay with us? I'd faced the same dilemma many times before with rescued hoglets, but somehow always managed to pull myself together and do the best thing for the animals, however fond I had become of them.

It was simply that Michael was different. Not only was he quite remarkably tame, but he was apparently perfectly content, never attempting to escape or showing those frantic surges of restlessness often seen in captive hedgehogs. Lying awake at night, I unwisely allowed my over-fertile imagination to run riot. It was all too easy to visualise our prickly friend faced with the many hazards that lie in wait for hedgehogs in the wild.

When I really stop to think, it absolutely flabbergasts me that *Erinaceus europaeus* has survived at all, with the odds so heavily against him. I find it heartbreaking that around one hundred thousand are killed or badly injured on our roads each year, while many more die in the nest or during their first hibernation.

I have to admit that I am one of those totally batty types who undoubtedly cause huge irritation to other motorists at night over the summer, by pootling along at about 10 m.p.h., eyes glued to the road ahead in search of kerb-crawling hogs in need of rescue or assistance. In short, a sort of mobile lollipop lady for hedgehogs. Yet, by being vigilant, I have rescued many road hogs and probably saved quite a few lives.

When I was very small, Nanny's light-hearted and tactful explanations of the all-too-frequent sightings of flattened hogs was that they were simply 'prickly pancakes', and nothing to worry myself about. As I was a tremendous devotee of Beatrix Potter, Nanny, foreseeing my reactions had I twigged that 'prickly pancakes' were slaughtered Tiggy-winkles, persisted in her wise deception until I was old enough to handle the awful truth.

Sometimes I think there are only two kinds of people in the world, those who try to avoid running over hedgehogs and those who don't. It is one of my worst nightmares that I should run over one myself. How people can run them over deliberately I just don't know, but they do. I've seen them. To be fair, one has to admit that hedgehogs are tricky to circumnavigate when you are buzzing along at 60 m.p.h. on a dark night and suddenly encounter a hog parked in the middle of the Queen's highway, while they are even harder to avoid if in the act of executing an ill-advised sprint from one side of the road to the other. A hedgehog in full throttle can't half move. In fact, they can run as fast as we can walk, but with a little care and extra vigilance, they may be avoided. As for those 'humans' who seem to delight in using hedgehogs for deliberate target practice, I can only say that such people must surely boast the I.Q. of your average syphilitic peahen, and are utterly beneath contempt.

Quite apart from murderous motorists, hedgehogs have to contend with numerous other dangers. Cattle-grids are lethal, though thanks to the splendid Major Adrian Coles, who invented escape ramps and went on to form the British Hedgehog Preservation Society, many hedgehogs have been spared a slow and lingering death. Bonfires, uncovered drains and water-butts, plastic-sided garden ponds, tennis nets and garden netting, broken glass, litter and household rubbish, the list is endless and, while the vision of a demented hog rushing madly to and fro with an empty yoghurt pot jammed over its face may be quite amusing in theory, in practice, it could well be fatal for the hog. Stubble-burning, low hedge-cutters, droughts and flooding are all equally dangerous. Of mother nature's natural predators, foxes, dogs and badgers certainly account for not a few, while rats may occasionally quite fancy a baby hedgehog for tea, and may even have a crack at a hibernating adult. As far as we know, magpies are the only feathered hedgehog predators.

It is rather a comfort to know that hedgehog-like creatures first trudged the earth millions of years ago, though fossilised remains record that this prehistoric Tiggy-winkle was not in fact clad in the usual spines. A type of hedgehog was certainly snoutling around in an idyllic motorway-free Britain about two million years ago, where one assumes that their only real concerns were coping with the odd Ice Age and avoiding being trodden on by a passing mammoth.

Around five million years ago, hedgehogs were to be found in every corner of the earth, except Australia, South America, Madagascar and Antarctica. Hedgehog fossils have been unearthed in North America, but for some obscure reason they did not survive there. One ancient specimen actually grew to about the size of a badger, and must have been quite an intimidating chap. Other fossilised remains tell us that another early variety of equal stature was a giant hairy model which lived in Italy and possibly grew to his impressive size on a diet of delicious prehistoric pasta! Hedgehogs are also known to have lived in early China, and were much revered in some provinces, while there is considerable archaeological evidence that our spiky friends were also to be found in ancient Egypt.

Our British hedgehog, having survived a chilly succession of Ice Ages, suddenly found himself having to contend with man, who, as we well know, has proved a formidable foe for centuries. By now a self-confessed insectivore, and clad in recognisable spines, the hedgehog began to thrive.

Hedgehogs, as we know them today, were mentioned in dispatches by such eminent ancients as Aristotle and Aesop, and also Pliny the Elder, who appears to have been the instigator of certain unfounded and defamatory rumours. He claimed that hedgehogs were skilful and intrepid apple thieves, able to shin up trees to reach the fruit. Unfortunately for the hedgehog, this myth persists, though there are no records of anyone actually witnessing a marauding hog in the act of climbing a tree in pursuit of a nice Granny Smith or Golden Delicious.

As well as conferring on hedgehogs the damning reputation of apple thieves *par excellence*, the Romans actually had the brass neck to use the dried out skins of hedgehogs as combs to card out wool, while the poor little blighters were increasingly considered a very acceptable source of human food, and still were until quite recently by certain sections of the travelling community! Nothing more tasty than a nice baked hedgehog for tea ... the mind boggles .... though I suppose it could be considered a bit of a change from a baked potato! .... but let us not be flippant.

Up to around the 15th century, the so-called 'men of medicine' regarded the hedgehog as a cure for certain maladies, though, as far as I know, history does not actually record in what way other than that they were supposed to cure tummy upsets. One cannot help imagining the possible result of swigging a brew of spiced hedgehog urine with a view to curing a tiresome ague, or the somewhat uncomfortable application of powdered hedgehog spines to one's housemaid's knee or tennis elbow.

By the middle ages the hedgehog had become something of a household name. Rumours and legends abounded and superstition was rife. Folk genuinely believed that hedgehogs sucked milk from the udders of cows and purloined whole crops of apples by rolling over and impaling them upon their spines prior to a jolly good guzzle out of sight of the irate apple farmer, whose very living depended on his crop.

Hedgehogs appeared on heraldic devices and family crests. Many a knight is known to have taken part in his local gymkhana or ridden into battle with several hedgehogs rampant upon his shield, or banner. Hedgehogs were seen in glorious technicolour in early stained glass windows, but despite this seemingly divine recognition, the species continued to be much maligned and persecuted. A certain Mr William Shakespeare did nothing to help by adding several exceedingly derogatory

'An apple thief par excellence...'

references to the hedgehog to his otherwise quite entertaining plays, where unflattering digs are made about 'urchins' and 'hedgepigs'. Immortal bard he may have been, but he certainly does not appear to have been a hedgehog fancier!

The Middle Ages were, on the whole, a less than happy time for hedgehogs. In 1566 Parliament actually put a price on the head of any hedgehog unfortunate enough to be captured, while so-called 'Mother Church' offered a reward for any hedgehog apprehended on church land. Bounties were put on hedgehogs rather like the 'baddies' in cowboy films, but eventually an act was passed to end this.

Quite suddenly, the hedgehog was regarded as rather a good chap to have around. Many great houses kept hedgehogs in their cellars to keep cockroaches and other juicy vermin at bay, while gardeners suddenly twigged that slugs, snails, beetles and other garden nuisances vanished with considerable alacrity were a hedgehog to take up residence on their patch. Then in 1833, a certain Professor Lorenz Oken saw the light and recommended that the hedgehog be officially protected; this, thankfully, is now the case in many countries but, strangely enough, not in Britain.

We think that there are about eleven recognised species of hedgehog on the loose to date. These inhabit the continents of Europe, Asia and Africa. In 1870 they were formally introduced to South Island, New Zealand, with further consignments of emigratory hogs being shipped out in 1885 and 1892. They were also introduced to North Island in 1910 to see if they approved of the place and would acclimatise. They obviously liked what they saw, and are now happily established, while the New Zealanders are only too pleased to have them, as they put paid to various major pests such as moths and grass grubs.

New Zealanders also feel kindly disposed towards these spiky immigrants as, for some reason, they do not harbour the rather unattractive hedgehog flea. There are two variety of hedgehog in New Zealand, the hairy and the spined. Both have the same anatomy and metabolism, but differ quite a bit in appearance.

After the last war *Erinaceus europaeus*, quite suddenly and after much persecution, came into its own. Hedgehogs became the 'in' thing and began to enjoy much welcome interest and publicity. They appeared on postage stamps, banners and logos, and the excellent work started off by Beatrix Potter spread to other authors, who immediately started to churn out books about hedgehogs, in particular for children. Artists and wild-life photographers, spotting a lucrative, if not prickly, opening in the market, set to and produced vast quantities of erinacean likenesses on greetings cards, calendars and wrapping paper. The soft toy industry also cashed in, producing thousands of cuddly hedgehogs, usually dressed in woolly hats and gaudy scarves. These were an instant hit with the tinies, especially at Christmas, when they appeared in droves clad in Santa Claus hats and plastic wellies. Documentaries on the hedgehog were seen regularly on the telly, thus educating and enlightening the great British public about the ways of the charming *Erinaceus europaeus*.

We in Britain are fortunate to play host to an extensive population of hedgehogs, though most areas above the 60th parallel do not have indigenous populations. Hedgehogs have been introduced to some northern islands, though dedicated observers report that, while some of these introduced colonies do not seem to be doing so well, others thrive, like those on North Ronaldsay in the Orkneys and Alderney in the Channel Islands.

Quite apart from obvious things like prickles, I personally find everything about the hedgehog appealing. They are such a nice shape for a start. The skull is somewhat shorter and blunter than that of most insectivores, with the cheek bones wide and strong.

An adult hedgehog boasts no fewer than thirty-six small teeth, typical of an insectivore, and, unlike those of carnivores, the canine teeth are hardly noticeable. The erinacean snout is also very insectivoreal, being pointed and exceedingly mobile. The nostrils open very much to the side which enables the hog to root around without bunging up its nasal passage. The average healthy nose is usually damp and may even appear a trifle runny, so lest you be tempted to wade in with a kleenex, it should perhaps be noted that damp or runny noses are quite normal, with the dampness actually enhancing the sense of smell.

Hedgehogs are strictly nocturnal, and I reckon that a good percentage of those spotted out and about in daylight are not totally happy for some reason. As I mentioned before, they are colour-blind and their eyesight is poor, though the eyes are quite big and very dark, protruding slightly, and are really quite shiny. As for ears, these are not very obvious in most species, except the desert variety, which possesses quite large and eye-catching specimens, and seems to be under the misapprehension that it is a sort of rabbit! Hedgehogs hear very well, at least as well as we humans, though they are not able to pick up high-frequency sounds such as those made by bats.

'Quite at home with humans ...'

While on a package holiday in Majorca a couple of years ago, I was delighted to discover that there was a family of native hedgehogs staying at the same hotel as us. Mum and three babies appeared each evening to stroll in the warm air, and avail themselves of the hotel rubbish heap where, if they were careful and didn't get a lager can stuck over their heads, the gastronomic delights were endless and there for the taking. I saw the mother the first night we were there, jogging along amidst the bougainvillaea, a smug expression on her face and half a cheeseburger clenched in her teeth. The hedgehogs were quite at ease with us and I was able to get a close look. These are Algerian hedgehogs, a bit smaller than our European model. The ears are quite a bit larger and the legs longer. They are not as dark as our hogs, and the spines are less close together. Altogether, quite smart little fellows, with an eye-catching white underside and longer snout.

I never realised what long legs hedgehogs possess until I saw Michael Heselspine standing up on tiptoe one evening in an attempt to climb up the side of the hamster cage. In fact, the legs are particularly long for such a plump body, about four inches in a mature adult, and make a rapidly-moving hedgehog look like a cross between a hairbrush on wheels and a spiky hovercraft. When the hog is foraging, the legs are tucked underneath to enable it to amble about; when elongated, they help the hedgehog to get up a bit of speed. Hedgehogs have flat feet and put the whole of the foot on the ground. I often think they look as if they are wearing rather elderly carpet slippers, especially on the hind feet. They have five toes and prominent pads on all feet which leave obvious tracks. The front feet turn slightly inwards and the back ones outwards. Each toe ends in a long and very serviceable claw, especially prominent on the hind feet. The middle three claws on the latter are especially handy for grooming, while the digging for food and nesting materials is done with the front feet.

I'm often asked how on earth I manage to pick up hedgehogs minus gloves, without getting impaled. Once you have acquired the knack and have a bit of practice under your belt, it is actually quite easy. The spines and hair around the head and face are particularly sensitive, while the underside of the hog is soft, hairy and free of prickles. In order to transport your hedgehog by hand from A to B insert both hands slowly beneath the hog in question, with your palms uppermost, thus coming into contact with the nice soft hairy part. If you are careful and persevere, most hogs will relax, stick their heads out, and paddle happily with their hind feet. Should the hog prove at all ticklish, it will probably collapse in a fit of giggles as well. Hedgehogs do so appreciate humans who move slowly and quietly and handle them with care, and warm especially to those who do not drop them. Suspicious nervy humans are strongly advised to wear gloves and hold the hog over some form of soft landing. This is particularly advisable if the hog in transit is of an equally nervous temperament, and has rolled into a tight unrelenting ball.

Erinacean romance has long been a source of great fascination to me. I once observed two fully grown hogs of opposite gender bobbing to each other, twirling round, and performing what looked like a pre-nuptial twosome-reel. These manoeuvres continued for fully twenty minutes before the larger of the two, almost certainly the prospective bride, got brassed off and wandered away grunting and huffing to herself, in a way that rather suggested boredom and lack of marital commitment. Her swain, meanwhile, stayed put, peering round in a bemused sort of way before giving chase at a considerable lick. One

'Standing up on tip-toe...'

could only speculate about the culmination of this somewhat unsatisfactory courtship, and hope that love eventually won the day.

For those of my readers who have survived thus far and who are remotely interested in the basic nitty gritty, the male hedgehog or 'boar' harbours the statutory bits of male equipment in the middle of his stomach, the testes being stored discreetly away inside the body. The chap is usually a little smaller than his lady friends, or 'sows', who flaunt their naughty bits somewhat brazenly for all to see, directly in front of the anal opening.

When a satisfactory 'conjugal visit' is in full swing, the sow obligingly lays her spines flat (much, I suspect to the relief of her suitor), stands quite still and sticks out her soft furry rear-end beyond the spines so that the boyfriend can, if he is still in a fit state, insert his impressively lengthy penis and, with any luck, put her in the family way. The usual litter of four or five is born between May and July, though second litters may arrive from August to September. Sadly, it is many of these later litters that will not survive the winter, unless they have reached at least a pound in weight, and preferably a bit more. The hoglets are born about five weeks after mating, and the mother should not be disturbed or she may desert her brood.

Ideally, the lifespan of a hedgehog should be as much as ten years, about a third of this being taken up with hibernation. Sadly, with all the hazards of modern life, most hedgehogs are lucky to survive for a couple of years.

Besides the hedgehog, there are other creatures who sport a covering of prickles. For example, the engaging echidna of

Australia and New Guinea is very similar and frequently called the Australian hedgehog, despite the fact that it is actually a monotreme or egg-laying mammal. Porcupines, found in all five continents, are considerably larger but are very like hedgehogs, though they are rodents and largely vegetarian. A mature European hedgehog can measure 23-25 centimetres when fully elongated. Ideally, a full grown hog should weight about 1½ - 2 lbs. and needs to be at its heaviest immediately prior to hibernation, with a good layer of brown fat on board, about a third of which will be lost while the hedgehog is asleep.

Hedgehogs are not social by nature; by that I mean that on the whole, they are solitary and do not live in groups. Babies will stay with mamma for about five weeks, after which they are quite ready to 'go it alone', as it were, and launch off on their own. Newly mated couples do not stay together after the nuptials and the boar takes no part in the rearing of the hoglets.

Hedgehogs do not appear to maintain a clearly defined territory or follow regular routes, and a mature male may cover as much as two miles during the nocturnal hours, while the sow tends to clock up a slightly lesser mileage. Their usual habitat includes gardens, fields, pasturelands and woodland, though many more are being recorded in town gardens, city cemeteries and parks, where, along with foxes and badgers, they seem to thrive.

I remember once winning quite a passable bottle of brandy in a general knowledge quiz, being the only one who knew how many spines one might expect to find on a hedgehog. My fellow contestants seemed quite foxed by this question, and I had the feeling that they viewed me as precisely the sort of crackpot who might well go out and waylay a passing hedgehog for the sole purpose of painstakingly counting every last prickle. I must confess that I still cannot work out how they do know how many prickles there are. No doubt, like most other things these days, its all done by computer. Somehow, the idea of a computerised hedgehog makes me feel a trifle uneasy.

A mature hedgehog has between 5,000 and 7,000 spines. These are creamy beige with a dull brown band, and afford the hedgehog very good camouflage. The actual spine is about an inch long, having a bulbous end which is hidden beneath the skin. The spines are incredibly strong and not only act as shock absorbers, should the hog have a fall, but are a splendid protection from cold and predators. Each individual spine has its own private muscle which is, in turn, attached to one big sheet of muscle that lines the hedgehog's back. This muscle is called the Panniculus Carnosus. If undamaged, some spines may stay in place for as long as two years. New-born hoglets have a few white spines, which increase in number and turn brown at three weeks old. Albino hedgehogs are uncommon, but do occur. These have the characteristic pink eyes and usually a pink nose to match, and though I feel the overall effect could be quite appealing, it is thought that few survive, being too conspicuous and often less robust than their brown relatives.

Apart from shedding the odd spine here and there, which is replaced in time, hedgehogs, luckily for them, do not go through a yearly moult. If they did, not only would they look exceedingly plain for some weeks, but would also be quite defenceless. Should you, perchance, happen upon a bald hedgehog, do try not to bolt in panic; it is not, as you might understandably assume, a haggis on the run; the poor little chap probably has ringworm, which can be treated by a sympathetic vet using Imaverol baths and a course of Griseovan tablets. Curing ringworm can take some weeks, but is most rewarding in the long run, as no self-respecting hedgehog cares to be seen in public minus his prickles.

When annoyed or frightened, the hedgehog is able to roll itself up into what may best be described as a spiky bag. The head and rump-end are tugged down hard and the whole operation is completed when another muscle called the Musculus Orbicularis is tightened. All the prickles become sharply erect, each pointing in a different direction and making the hedgehog more or less impregnable.

I once saw a rather aggressive dachshund going absolutely spare with frustration at coming upon a tightly rolled ball of exceedingly sharp and inhospitable prickles which no amount of Germanic guile could undo. On another occasion, I spotted two beastly little boys using a tightly rolled hedgehog as a football. Needless to say, I pounced with such verbal fury that the two little horrors fled instantly. To be sure, the queen in *Alice in Wonderland* did use a hedgehog for a croquet ball, but croquet is a somewhat more refined game than soccer, and I'm glad to report that the above mentioned 'football' was quite unharmed and very soon sauntered off after a quick check-up from me.

When people come to our house, they seldom get a chance to retreat without being offered both a cup of tea or coffee and an invitation to come and see Michael Heselspine. In nine cases out of ten, the invitation is accepted with alacrity. Visitors are ushered out into the garden having first been briefed as to how one conducts oneself in the presence of a celebrity like Michael. For the most part, these audiences are a great success, especially round about evening when Michael is on the move. Ever ready to impress a would-be fan, he can usually be relied upon to put on a bit of a show. Most people take to him at once, and I can see why, but then, of course, I'm biased. His appeal is obvious, even to the more nervous and unindoctrinated *Erinaceus* fan. However, I have to say that this is not always the case. I have known the odd less hog-minded visitor react in a negative way.

One old trout physically recoiled at the sight of Michael's hairy face and carpet-slipper feet as I held him out for closer inspection, while another announced that she wouldn't dream of harbouring such a smelly flea-ridden object in the bosom of HER family. There seemed little point in assuring her that he was not in the least smelly, just faintly aromatic, and that I'd never waylaid a single flea on him yet. On this particular occasion, Michael repaired swiftly to his bed, and the rather frightful visitor, who didn't like Jack Russells either, and therefore should never have got past the front door anyhow, was shown out without further ado.

Eventually, I suppose that I will have to accept that there are people around who simply do not like animals. Full stop. Ian constantly has to remind me that I really must not automatically assume that everyone is as batty as I am about most varieties of fish, fowls and furries.

It has occurred to me that I may take it all just a little too far sometimes. Things like going out for long solitary walks while the Grand National is being shown live on the telly. I simply cannot watch it for fear of seeing those lovely horses crashing earthwards. Instead I stomp off through the woods muttering heartfelt prayers for equine deliverance and will only watch the re-run if I can be assured that none of the horses has been injured or killed. Deliberate cruelty to any animal produces an instant and often explosive reaction. Once, while on holiday in Morocco, I spotted a hefty and somewhat unsavoury looking Arab belabouring a tiny spindly donkey who was struggling desperately to pull a hopelessly overloaded cart. Quite without contemplating the possible repercussions, I set about the tur-baned brute with verbal and physical fury, and it was only the timely intervention of our tour guide that prevented me from being carted off to a Marrakesh jail.

Though not excessively partial to spiders (especially those en-sconced on Australian loo seats), we have one, name of Chumley, who resides, on and off, in our bath. He seems a pleasant sort of chap, and appears content to squat in a plastic tooth-mug while we humans ablute, after which he is returned to his dwelling place. I do not desperately take to snakes ei-ther, nor some of the less well mannered species of monkey; but cannot for the life of me understand how anyone could not possibly find the hedgehog anything other than totally enchant-ing, with Michael Heselspine an excellent ambassador for his kind.

Chapter IV

The Best Of Breeds

Does your hot-water bottle snore? Mine does. It also takes up considerably more room than your average hot-water bottle, requires the periodical check-up for leaks, is apt to change gear just as you are about to drop off to sleep, and has been known to emit highly aromatic though, thankfully, non-toxic gases at odd intervals throughout the night.

Though still unrecognised by the Kennel Club, despite much lobbying from their numerous devotees, Jack Russells have many and varied talents, quite apart from making excellent hot-water bottles. Among these is the unfailing ability to hog the limelight, not to mention the duvet, and remain annoyingly cheerful against all odds.

Mippy came to us in a great hurry, being, at the time, under sentence of instant death at the hands of an irate gun-toting gamekeeper whose pheasant chicks she had allegedly been harassing. Her first owner, an elderly lady, had doted on her, stuffed her with Turkish delight and generally spoilt her rotten; as she was hardly ever allowed off the lead, and therefore seldom got out of first gear, she was, as a result, extremely stout. When the old lady died, Mippy was immediately put on a strict diet by the old dear's somewhat formidable cleaning lady, with whom she was forced to take up temporary residence until a new owner could be persuaded to take her on.

From the moment she arrived on our door step, Mippy endeared herself to us with her stocky little body, jaunty ears and cheerful expression. After two days she had us hooked, and totally committed to the continuous overseeing of her comfort and well-being. We have no idea how old she is. The suggestion from Ian, that we should try cutting her in half and counting the rings, is received with howls from Lucy.

She is what Ian ominously describes as an 'Oven Ready' Jack Russell, being on the plump side rather than fat. He has a way of rolling her over onto her back with all four feet in the air, then picking her up and holding her aloft as though she were on a silver platter and about to be served up at a medieval banquet. Mippy, far from resenting this, seems to enjoy the attention, though I have occasionally felt it prudent to intervene as the conversation veers towards gravy and stuffing etc. and ominous queries such as 'which end did I think we should insert the onion!'

Mippy excels in most of the things that Jack Russells are generally reckoned to be good at. The dedication with which she will keep favourite armchairs warm for us is indeed touching, while eagle-eyed supervision of family meals, the issuing of endless irresistible invitations to 'walkies', coupled with her undeniable advantages as a built-in bed warmer, would surely melt the heart of even the most anti-Jack Russell person.

Lucy adores her, and Mippy returns this feeling a hundredfold. Trotting after Lucy everywhere, she even allows herself to be treated like a doll or much loved teddy bear. Surely there is no more beguiling sight than a small brown and white dog lying back happily in a doll's pram clad in Care Bear pyjamas, and bobble hat?

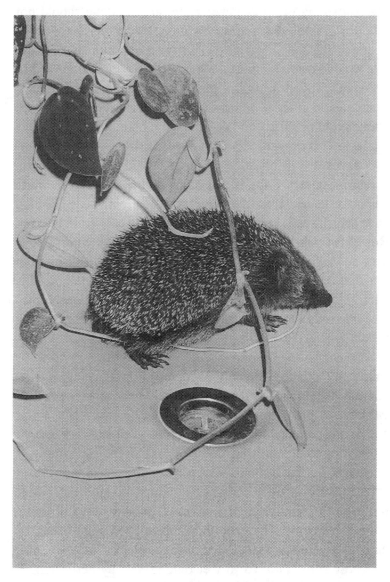

'Pottering in our avocado bath ...'

Over the six years that she has owned us, I have been forced to point out to Mippy on numerous occasions that Jack Russells are something of an acquired taste, and that she should not take for granted that everyone she encounters has necessarily acquired this taste. My misgivings over her unquenchable desire to love every human who comes through the door and to be equally loved in return, have remained. She, in her turn, continues to greet all comers with loud and joyful yells, much animated jumping up, and determined monopolisation of visiting laps. This show of 'do-it-yourself' Jack Russell PR inevitably leaves a trail of laddered tights, smudged Lizzy Arden, creased Country Casuals and navy cardies covered in white hairs. Amazingly, these demonstrations of irrepressible affection have actually been known to produce the odd convert to the Jack Russell fan club. Inevitably, however, there are a scattering of hardened and self-confessed non-Jack Russell people who retreat from our house convinced that their original opinion of the breed is entirely justified, and that all Jack Russells are unquestionably perfect little sods. On the whole we find we get to count more of the former among our friends, than the latter.

Like many others, I roundly condemned the docking of tails, and am delighted that this barbaric and unnecessary practice has been stopped, more or less. Can you imagine being a dog and having nothing to wag? To see a totally tail-less Jack Russell attempting to demonstrate delight is heart-rending. I know of one living not far from us who, besides being well on in years and distinctly portly to boot, has absolutely no tail whatsoever, not even the semblance of a stump. How any vet could have done it beats me - he must either have been blind drunk or harboured deep and vindictive feelings against Jack Russells. The little soul is forced to welcome friends by performing a rather quaint 'rumba' with her chubby white rear, which invariably produces mirth from passing humans and sideways glances from any male dog who happens to be in the vicinity.

One favourite Jack Russell of my acquaintance is Bertie Proctor, who lives just up from us. Bertie is definitely one of nature's gentlemen, being consistently friendly to all he meets, and particularly partial to lady Jack Russells and pussy-cats. He is also the proud owner of an exceedingly splendid tail, some twelve inches in length, which he carries jauntily like a sort of hairy question mark over his back.

Among Bertie's many talents, precision defecation must surely take pride of place. I well remember watching with undisguised admiration as Bertie, with deep concentration, lined himself up, and with a measured glance over his shoulder, slowly and deliberately reversed up to one of my more eye-catching shrub tubs and deposited an undeniably spectacular turd, smack in the middle of a rather impressive hosta. His elderly owner, who had dropped in for coffee, was quite overcome with embarrassment and threatened immediate corporal punishment, while I was enchanted, despite the desecration of my hosta, and quite unable to utter even a word of reproach.

Lucy was fearfully impressed, needless to say, and 'Dirty Bertie' Proctor was noticeably satisfied with his achievement. The act had been so meticulously planned, and executed with such unerring accuracy and panache, that I couldn't have been angry if I'd tried, and was forced to reflect that only a Jack Russell could have got away with such outrageous behaviour.

Comparisons between Bertie and Mippy are interesting. Apart from the fact that both are Jack Russells, they are quite dissimilar in appearance. Bertie, whose third cousin four times

'Jack Russells do get on with hedgehogs sometimes....!'

74

removed, on his mother's side, could well have been a bit of a mixture, is larger and more hairy, while Mippy is small and quite compact, and as Lucy quite rightly observes, distinctly like a piggy-bank. Where tails are concerned, Bertie flaunts the previously described hairy question mark, while Mippy is adequately equipped with an expressive and easily manipulated four-inch stump. As for legs, while both dogs possess the requisite four apiece, Bertie's are unquestionably of the Hepplewhite persuasion, Mippy's being instantly recognisable as Queen Anne, especially the front ones. Regarding ears, Bertie's are definitely 'pipistrelle' while Mippy's are more of your 'fruit bat', particularly when they are standing vertically in anticipation of a chocolate digestive.

More than any other breed, I seem to count more Jack Russells among my acquaintances than any other. Our local pet shop is run by one, name of Nipper Martin, a black, white and brown young chap with a built-in grin. Nipper stands with his back legs on a chair and his front ones on the counter welcoming all prospective customers. He is particularly agreeable to those who assume he is for sale, and come in to enquire the price, and chats amiably to members of the public who pop in for a bag of doggy-bics or a pound of bunny-mix. Meanwhile his owners, apparently content to hand over the front-of-house side of things to Nipper, beaver away in the background doing all the donkey work involved in running a busy pet shop. Were he human, Nipper would almost certainly wear a tweed cap over one eye, converse in broad cockney, and be a top-notch salesman able to sell anything to anyone on charm alone.

Our area seems to abound with Jack Russells of particular character, and while most of them are pillars of society and respectability, a small minority manage to achieve a slightly less admirable reputation. Double-barrelled or hyphenated Jack Russells are, to my mind, usually confirmed rakes and philanderers. Such a one is Boswell Boyd-Brent. Bos, as he is usually known, is a positive flashman among Jack Russells. Altogether the sort of likeable bounder who would think nothing of scoffing a whole box of After Eights at 7.30! Allowed to come and go more or less as he pleases, he saunters the streets of our small town exuding debonair self-confidence and manages to ingratiate himself with nearly everyone he encounters. When I say 'nearly everyone' I intend to convey, as tactfully as I can, that Boswell does, very occasionally, rub people up the wrong way. For starters, he is a self-confessed Don Juan, and will pursue absolutely any canine of the female gender, no matter how elderly or unattractive. He is often to be found sitting determinedly on the front doorsteps of irritated owners of 'fascinating ladies', and is not above the odd nocturnal serenade below a loved one's window. The very fact that he is more of a 'Mick Jagger' than a 'Placido Domingo' does nothing at all to endear him to the sleeping public.

One of Boswell's more anti-social pastimes is his persistent desire to imitate a traffic cop. At tremendous risk, not only to his own life but also to those of others, he thinks nothing of striding into the centre of the busy high street, there to stand with all the immovability of a concrete bollard, while the traffic grinds to a halt and the entire street ends up in one hell of a traffic jam. I myself, who know his owners well, have waded in and conveyed him back to the pavement several times, thus enabling the town to return to some semblance of normality

One day, all hell was let loose. Boswell's charming but rather scatty owners found themselves on the receiving end of a possible court action if they did not immediately undertake to keep

Bos under control and restrict his less appealing activities. Foremost among the 'Down with Boswell' lobby was the owner of a local hotel and restaurant, a somewhat posh establishment whose frontage Boswell was wont to frequent. This gentleman went so far as to announce that, should he observe the Boswellian hind leg cocked against his high-class potted conifers one more time, the legal axe would fall. The upshot of all this was that poor Boswell was thereafter tethered on a very long string that just enabled him to sit on the pavement outside his front gate. Here members of the public, soppy enough to be taken in by the doleful expression and tail at half mast, would stop to commiserate.

Since I started on this little book, Boswell has moved house, and is now the contented custodian of a rambling country mansion that his owners are hoping to renovate. It goes awfully well with his double-barrelled name, is miles from any road, not to mention testy restaurateurs, and he has quite taken to his new role of canine country squire.

In most respects, Mippy is a spunky little wench, but when it comes to visiting the vet, she is an appalling coward. Thankfully, we don't need to bother the vets that often, but on the odd occasion that we do have to go to the surgery, the entire place knows about it. Mippy, the veterinary staff and myself, are all reduced to gibbering wrecks at the mere thought of her yearly booster shot, and as for having her toenails cut, she screeches like a demented banshee at the sight of the clippers.

I recently took Mippy to the vet's to have her M.O.T. Lucy volunteered to come along too, more, I suspect in the hope of witnessing an interesting fracas than out of any great desire to support Mum. Initially all went well: no injections, tooth extractions, enemas or amputations required, and we prepared to depart. The beady-eyed vet, however, had spotted a couple of small round swellings on Mippy's chest. Gently he had a feel and examined the bumps. "I know exactly what those are," said Lucy, always ready to help a vet in distress. "Oh," said our good-natured vet, who had kiddies of his own, "and what do you think they are?" "Hairy bosoms, of course," announced Lucy in a tone that indicated that she did rather feel that, after long years studying at the Royal Dick, the vet should possibly have reached the obvious himself. The dear boy appeared hugely impressed, and declared that of course Lucy was absolutely spot-on, and that he was most grateful for her assistance with what could well have been a tricky diagnosis. Mippy, meanwhile, was still up on the table, quite rigid with apprehension. The bumps turned out to be quite harmless fatty deposits, common in the more mature and somewhat corpulent models, but I had to admit that they did look for all the world like hairy bosoms. Were they to get bigger, as the vet hinted they well might, I did feel that a quick dash to Marks and Spencer's bra department might eventually be the order of the day.

The other thing that Mippy thoroughly dislikes is snow. Being somewhat short in the leg, with her tummy in close proximity to the ground, she finds that to be out in more than three inches for longer than about five seconds, is, to say the least, unpleasant. Clad in the chopped-off sleeve of Lucy's old school cardie with holes cut for her legs, she really only consents to go out in the snow when the desire to jettison excess fuel can no longer be ignored. Her back view on these occasions speaks volumes. Every step is an effort. The ears and tail droop to their lowest possible ebb, and the gait can only be compared to that of a cross between a duck with piles and a penguin wearing a very wet nappy. The entire picture is one of sheer and utter misery, and she's back inside before you can say 'knife'.

Like most Jack Russells, Mippy is incredibly greedy. She will eat just about everything on offer and is particularly partial to spaghetti hoops and Cadbury's cream eggs. She consumes her own dinner with lightning speed and, if not intercepted, everyone else's as well. Lucy finds Mippy most useful, a sort of canine disposal unit, and unwanted Ready Brek, fish fingers or peanut butter sandwiches that have outlived their appeal are all polished off with great alacrity by Mippy, always delighted to help out in times of crisis.

Mippy's obsession with pleasures gastronomic very nearly proved fatal on one occasion, however. I had purchased several of those very thick solid dogmeat sausages encased in tough polythene, one of which is supposed to feed a dog for about a week. The sausages were stored away in a cupboard out of reach, or so we thought, of plundering Jack Russells. Alas, we were wrong, for somehow Mippy managed to get hold of one with what might well have been fatal consequences. We were out for a couple of hours, and I suppose that Mippy, understandably with an eye to the main chance, decided that our temporary absence gave her the time and incentive to embark on a little discreet sausage hunting.

On arriving home, we were confronted by what could only be described as a cross between Jimmy Knapp and a Zeppelin on legs standing immobile in the middle of the floor, apparently quite unable to move. She looked exactly as though she had been blown up with a bicycle pump and was only in a fit state to roll her eyes and burp. Off to the vet we shot, with Mippy for once unable and unwilling to offer any form of resistance, verbal or physical.

The vets were quite enthralled, and at one stage there were three of them, plus the lady who does the typing and makes the coffee, standing round admiring our spectacularly inflated Jack Russell and uttering exclamations of disbelief and amazement. The general consensus of opinion was that it was nothing short of a miracle that Mippy hadn't actually burst, and the most senior partner announced that in nearly twenty years of practice, he had never seen anything like it.

It took Mippy four days to deflate. The vet assured us cheerfully that she would, in all probability, succumb to chronic diarrhoea and be exceedingly sick, after which, all would be back to normal. Not a bit of it. She neither vomited nor squittered, but merely went down slowly and imperceptibly like a pricked balloon, sitting immobile in her basket with a soul-destroying expression of discomfort on her face, while emitting a more or less constant flow of deflationary sound effects from either end. You'd have thought she'd have learnt her lesson - not she. Once restored to her normal circumference, she was every bit as gluttonous as before. The remaining 'sausages' were placed on a shelf at least ten feet from the ground.

Jack Russells are generally reckoned to be keen and efficient hunters. In most cases they probably are, given the right circumstances. Mippy, on the other hand, has never really excelled in that direction, though she does quite enjoy the thrill of the chase, preferably in very short bursts.

Vanishing briefly one day while out in the field behind our house, she re-appeared after some ten or so minutes bearing quite one of the largest rabbits I'd ever seen. Slowly and very laboriously she lugged it the length of the field to where I stood ready to congratulate her on her magnificent achievement, an accolade which I believed was justly deserved, especially as, to my knowledge, she had never before succeeded in apprehending anything larger than a grasshopper or possibly an adolescent frog.

The rabbit really was quite vast and from a distance looked more like a hare . She eventually staggered up to me with her prize and laid it triumphantly at my feet, before collapsing in an exhausted heap. It was only when I picked the rabbit up that I understood how Mippy had succeeded in capturing it. The late lamented bun was as stiff as a board and must have been dead all of three days. There wasn't a mark on it, and no sign of any myxomatosis. I could only assume that the poor chap, having reached his allotted span, must have died of natural causes. Meanwhile, Mippy's pride in her prize was a pleasure to see, and who was I to disillusion her?

The day that Mippy decided to run away and see the world was quite one of the worst of my life. She ran off into the thick woods near our house and simply disappeared off the face of the earth for six days. There one moment, gone the next. When she had not returned by the following morning, the entire village was roped in to search, local gamekeepers alerted, S.S.P.C.A. officials notified and 'lost' posters hastily knocked up by Lucy and depicting crayon drawings of lost Jack Russells with gloomy expressions, pinned up at the vet's, on trees and in the local shop.

It was the awful 'not knowing' that affected me most. I roamed the woods far into the nights, rather like some wild demented woman, yelling her name and hurling unprintable abuse at a bloody owl who apparently derived some satisfaction from accurate and oft-repeated imitations of a Jack Russell in distress.

At times like this, the imagination can run riot. It was all too easy to picture a tiny rotting corpse, white paws pointing heavenwards, floating down the nearby river. I visualised her imprisoned in a cage, awaiting a grisly fate at the hands of evil vivisectionists, or, worst of all, hammering frantically with ineffectual little feet on the windows of a speeding dormobile en route to live out her remaining days incarcerated in a high-rise council flat in Milton Keynes. It simply didn't bear thinking about. I all but went to pieces, leaving poor Ian convinced that total mental collapse was imminent.

For five nights we left the garden gate into the field propped open just wide enough to admit a tiny precious prodigal, but it was all to no avail; and then, on the morning of the sixth day, 'God suddenly re-invented Jack Russells' and the prayed-for miracle happened. It was Sunday, and I was slouching listlessly in bed with a large mug of Maxwell House and a slice of toast and marmalade, trying to rally myself sufficiently mentally and physically to go to church, in order to pray for canine deliverance.

Suddenly, there was a tremendous hullabaloo from the kitchen, shouts from Lucy, and much frenzied barking from the other dogs. I stayed where I was, hardly daring to breathe. The din came nearer, then into the room burst Lucy, clad in what had once been white pyjamas, bearing in her arms something that could only be described as a dirty pink, and rather skinny piglet. The 'piglet', on seeing me, wriggled out of Lucy's arms, landed on the bed and, sending the remains of my coffee flying, hurled itself on me, yelling in joy before diving beneath the duvet leaving a trail of sticky pink mud in its wake.

Almost inarticulate with joy and weeping copiously, I phoned our long-suffering vet, who, far from being shirty at being phoned at 7.30 am on a Sunday morning, was delighted at the good news and instantly agreed to meet me at the surgery in half an hour to check the wanderer over.

Mippy was absolutely plastered in muddy sandstone from the bank above our stretch of the River Tweed, hence the somewhat porcine colour. She had lost a lot of weight, was very dehydrated, and, so the vet declared, had almost certainly been stuck deep down a rabbit burrow. This would have accounted for the fact that we had not heard so much as a yelp during all the time she was lost. Apart from her filthy state and weight loss, she was unharmed and as overjoyed to be home as we were to have her back.

The vet advised a controlled diet for a few days, in order that her empty tummy might acclimatise once more to food. A little lightly boiled white fish cooked in milk might be tasty, and some chicken was recommended as well, with saucers of milk and glucose to wash it all down. Normally, Mippy would not altogether have taken to the idea of a 'controlled' diet. In her book, the less controlled the diet, the better; but this menu sounded rather nice, and she was more than happy to give it a go. Once bathed, and restored to her own comfortable colour again, Mippy proceeded to enjoy convalescence hugely, and rapidly returned to normal. Word of her return soon got around, and great was the feeling of relief among the locals that life was back to normal once more.

For my part, I never want to go through the same experience again. It left me an absolute nervous wreck. I rushed out and bought a 20-foot Flexilead so that Mippy, who had shown signs of wanderlust on other occasions, could enjoy plenty of scope for exercise with no chance of escape. My nerves, let alone anyone else's, could not have stood it.

On this occasion all had ended happily, but I knew that we had been lucky and that there could well have been a tragedy. Appropriately enough, it was our splendid vet who helped end the saga on a humorous note. Remarking dryly that, as Mippy had managed to lose so much weight as a result of being jammed in a rabbit hole for several days, did I not feel that this course of action, though drastic, might produce a similar result for me? Lucy declared this to be a great idea, and so much cheaper than Weight Watchers too. Could she not perhaps come, like A.A. Milne's Rabbit, and drape tea-towels across my legs, especially as I was distinctly Pooh-shaped; and, in any case, it would be rather fun.

It is on occasions like this that I thank God, yet again, for a sense of humour, and for the ability to find a funny side in most situations. Mippy was home. Everything was all right, and we were happy again.

Chapter V

All Sorts Of Things

I never thought that I'd actually admit that we have too many animals, but after the last head-count, I'm beginning to think that this may be the case. To date, we share our home with four dogs, one hamster, three rats, six guinea-pigs, two gold-fish, five rabbits, three hedgehogs, a brace of gerbils and a stick insect called Julian.

'RATS?' I hear you exclaim. 'How on earth could anyone in their right mind possibly want to keep rats?' Now up to a point I can understand these sentiments, but I have to say that, while firmly excluding your common wild rat, there are some quite appealing specimens of 'Rattus domesticus' around.

Some years ago, I acquired a very handsome young rat who had been advertised in our local paper, rather ominously, as 'surplus laboratory stock'. He was jet-black and had very prominent pink ears and an imposingly long tail. I called him 'General Amin' after a certain Ugandan War Lord who was somewhat notorious at the time. 'The General' was highly intelligent, friendly and quite manic about his tail, spending hours polishing and buffing it with his paws.

One day an old dear from up the road came knocking at my door brandishing a collecting box for the S.S.P.C.A. I put a couple of quid into her tin, and we were passing the time of day when I suddenly became aware that the colour was draining from her cheeks, while her eyes had taken on a slightly shell-shocked look. Letting out a strangled shriek, she fled up the path, and it was only then that I realised the reason for her apparent terror. 'The General', who was perched on my shoulder when the doorbell went, and whom I'd quite forgotten about, had poked his black face out from behind my then long hair, and had, not surprisingly, given the poor old soul one hell of a turn. She must have thought she was hallucinating or had finally entered senility, and it was interesting that, the following year she crept cautiously down my drive bearing a collecting box for the Lifeboat, having, I assumed, decided that rats were a less deserving cause than those in peril on the sea.

Among our three rats, two are really quite pleasant, while the third is perfectly foul. Bollinger and Beadle, usually known as the 'Ratty Boys', are, on the whole, quite affable chaps, though apt to be a wee bit smelly if not watched. Bollinger is a dark mahogany brown with a creamy tummy, while Beadle is pure white with pink accessories. They are litter brothers and are devoted to each other. We tend not to handle them as neither is beyond giving a sly nip, but they do give us quite a lot of amusement with their antics.

In fact, Beadle did have a crack at my little finger one day, but as there was some sliced carrot in his bowl at the time, I suspect it was more a case of mistaken identity that a desire to draw blood. Rats are a bit short-sighted, and I could see how the muddle might have occurred. Just to be on the safe side, I did phone the health centre to check on the tetanus situation. Most medical receptionists would have been thrown by an agitated patient phoning to announce that they had been bitten by Jeremy Beadle, and should they rush in for a tetanus? It was noticeable that, on hearing who the caller was, absolutely no surprise was registered at all, merely an enquiry as to what species of quadruped we were discussing this time.

Glenys, named after a certain parliamentary wife, though more usually known as 'Rat Bag', is infinitely less attractive both in looks and personality. She is a sort of pale lentil soup colour with shifty red eyes which follow you around the room, rather like the Mona Lisa's, but less friendly. Glenys, quite frankly, is thoroughly bad-tempered, and would amputate your finger at the first opportunity. She is only interested in two things, food and sex. Of the former, she gets an adequate amount when I pluck up sufficient courage to open her cage door wide enough to enable her to snatch it. Of the latter, she gets none. This, for two reasons, a) I simply couldn't cope with a further genera-tion of 'Rat Bags', particularly if they were to take after mother, and b) neither Bollinger nor Beadle is remotely interested, as they are far too devoted to each other to bother with Glenys. We did try introducing Glenys to Bollinger one day, before we realised quite how foul she really was, but it turned out to be a total non-starter. While poor old Glenys stood rigid with ex-pectancy, an anticipatory expression of lust on her face, Bollinger ambled nonchalantly round her cage, helping himself to the odd snack from her bowl, squatting in a corner for a quick widdle, and, though he did pause once to give her a some-what desultory sniff, was totally uninterested in the prospect of copulation. Actually I think that's probably what turned poor old 'Rat Bag' sour as she was noticeably evil-tempered and sulky from that day on. An excellent example of Hell hav-ing no fury like a Rat Bag scorned!

On the subject of rescues: about eighteen months ago, we heard of a whippet bitch, neglected and shut in a shed on an estate not far from us. After discreet enquiries, and some very under-cover detective work, we were tipped the wink that, unless someone waded in soon, she would certainly be a case for the S.S.P.C.A. A 'rescue plan' was put into action, and the unattractive and sullen owners were finally persuaded to part with her with the minimum of fuss.

Binny, or 'Bin-Bin' as we called her because of her deep affection for dustbins, is fawn and white, six years old, and was, when she first arrived, a bag of bones. As Lucy remarked, she looked like one of those kits you put together to make a dinosaur skeleton, all bumps and lumps, while her tail, a pathetic thing indeed, was more or less devoid of hair, and an anaemic pink. The vets were horrified, and at once put her on a special high-protein diet and lots of rather Smartie-like vitamin pills. Her history was more one of neglect and total lack of interest than outright cruelty. So sweet-tempered was she that we were pretty sure that she hadn't actually been physically abused, though, to my mind, shutting a thin-coated dog like a whippet in a draughty shed in winter, itself constitutes a degree of cruelty.

An hour after arriving, Bin-Bin and Mippy were curled up in a blissful heap on the sofa. Bin-Bin, having gulped down a good meal and three saucers of milk, was already beginning to feel that life was worth living again. By lunch-time the following day, it was as if she'd been with us all her life. I will never forget the vision of Bin-Bin sitting on the kitchen floor with Lucy, bedecked in a pink satin shawl with sequins on it, wearing a curly blond wig, property of the local drama club, and crowned with Lucy's mauve plastic bath-hat. A dab of blue eye-shadow over each eye, and a trace of pale pink lipstick added both colour and class. Looking rather like a cross between Ivana Trump and Yassir Arafat, and with a blissful expression on her face, she must indeed have thought she'd died and gone to heaven!!

If anything, Bin-Bin is even more obsessive about duvets than Mippy, and, if permitted, will hurtle into our bedroom in the morning and launch herself like an Exocet missile onto the bed and under the duvet. Unlike Jack Russells, whippets make unsatisfactory hot-water bottles. To start with, they have rather a lot of sharp bits, so that curling up with a whippet can feel a little like lying in close proximity to a folded camera tripod, while an early morning kiss from Bin-Bin is rather like being prodded with an ice lolly. I've got the hang of all this now, and once I've manoeuvred Bin-Bin's sharp bits so that they do not correspond with my soft bits and the 'ice lolly' has thawed out, it's actually quite soothing to cuddle up with a whippet. They do not seem to snore quite as loudly as Jack Russells, though they do occasionally produce sounds like a diving submarine when dreaming about fast-moving bunnies.

In cold weather, both Mippy and Bin-Bin will polish off a light breakfast, and then head for the newly vacated but still warm nuptial bed, where they dig in and stay doggo for anything up to three hours. As a result of this, I have become exceedingly proficient at making a large double bed without disturbing the unconscious canines within.

As her health improved and her energy returned, Bin-Bin began to amaze us with her agility and turn of speed. Lucy, who had already discovered that whippets have especially designed snouts, which are ideal for polishing up the very bottom of Pot Noodle containers, also spotted Bin-Bin's racing potential, built a course of quite impressive obstacles on the back patio, and soon had Bin-Bin in training for the Grand National. Urged on by encouraging yells of "biccy-time" from Lucy, she positively flew over the jumps, ears streaming behind like a sort of canine Red Rum, with Mippy, not to be outdone, belting along in her wake, though electing to tackle the jumps from below rather than above. So reckless did Bin-Bin become, leaping anything from barbed-wire fences to stationary cars, that I became a little weary of dashing to the vets to have her stitched up or bandaged. The ever-practical Lucy suggested that a few notices warning of 'low-flying whippets' might be appropriate, and would give the locals a chance to duck should they hear the sound of galloping paws approaching.

Bin-Bin's first summer with us was crowned with success and glory. She won quite a few rosettes at local dog shows, including a large and rather gaudy pink-and-purple one for the best rescued dog in her class. You'd have thought she had been going to shows all her life. She would mince into the ring with Lucy on the end of a lead, smile sweetly at the judge, and proceed to carry out a sort of advanced dressage test for whippets, causing the watching crowd, and usually the judge as well, to fall about in admiration. This show-stopping display almost always resulted in a rosette and quite often a bag of doggy bics as well.

It could be said that this new-found devotion to the whippet as a breed is apt to go just a mite too far. While on a visit to John Lewis's china and glass department in Edinburgh, I was browsing as usual amongst the china hedgehogs and Jack Russells, when I spotted a perfectly heavenly Border Fine Arts 'whippet'. So uncannily like Bin-Bin was it, it was as though the maker had used her as a model. I, needless to say, fell hook, line and sinker. Alas, on observing the price tag, my idyll was shattered as the whippet cost £85.00 and was way beyond my pocket at the time. Dolefully, I made my way to the somewhat less appealing undies department leaving the china whippet gazing sadly after me from her glass shelf.

Over the next six months I made several visits to John Lewis, lurking furtively in the china and glass department as I visited my friend who, rather to my surprise, had not been sold. It was a bit like visiting a dog's home and not being able to make up one's mind whether one could afford to rescue a dog or not. Each time I went, I felt sure she would be gone and, in a way, I rather hoped she would as the problem would have been solved once and for all; but she was always there, beaming at me from behind her glass wall.

Then, one day, while on a mission to top up Lucy's school knicker supply, I popped into the china department for my usual visit when I observed, to my horror, a thick-set surly looking geezer with a loo-brush hair cut and a ring in his ear, parked right next to my whippet. He quite definitely looked interested, so, without further ado, and having decided that he was precisely the sort of chap who probably tended to brow-beat real whippets, I flew to the sales lady and demanded her instant attention. Ten minutes later I was heading at a smart trot for the school knicker department with my whippet, safely stashed away in a box full of polystyrene balls, nestling in a John Lewis's carrier bag. The sales lady was terribly nice and turned out to be equally partial to whippets. When I admitted somewhat shamefacedly that I had been visiting the whippet for months, she said "how gorgeous", and knocked five quid off the price.

Quite the least attractive side of keeping four dogs is that one constantly has to clear up after them and, while I'm not squeamish, I do get somewhat irked with the endless tours, shovel in hand, to scoop up the numerous 'burnt offerings' that lie in wait in the garden. Ian has been known to observe that the whole garden is 'exactly like a ruddy minefield' and has been heard to mutter darkly about 'decrees-not-so-nisi' on going out to mow the lawn, only to find that yours truly has not yet been out on mine-sweeping patrol.

Pottering out to the garden one day, I encountered what could only be described as a total defecationary disaster. Reminding myself that, as far as I knew, we had not yet actually acquired an elephant, I simply could not imagine what could possibly have produced such huge and unusual heaps of dung. On close inspection they proved to contain considerable quantities of what I was quickly able to identify as dried mixed fruit. With suitable caution, in case we *had* acquired an elephant unbeknownst, I followed the trail and, on rounding a corner of the house, encountered the culprit in the very act. Not an elephant, but a painfully embarrassed whippet sitting on her potty in the middle of the lawn.

As he is considered a far better cake-maker than I, Ian had been asked by a local lady to bake a cake for the 'blind dogs' cake stall. A 500-gram bag of mixed dried fruit had unwisely been left out on the counter in the kitchen, and none of us had noticed that it had vanished. The other dogs were not apparently afflicted with similar dire consequences, and we realised to our horror that Bin-Bin must have guzzled the lot. I can only say that the spectacular results lasted four days. It was like watching a high-powered hosepipe in action. We did not punish her, any more than we had punished Mippy after the polythene sausage episode; the off-loading of recycled sultanas with little warning and at regular intervals was punishment enough, as the expression on Bin-Bin's face betrayed.

The cake ingredients passed through Bin-Bin with astounding

'In which Michael is entirely surrounded by owls...'

'Do you come here often...?'

'Conversing with some china frogs...'

'A rather fierce-looking plastic lobster...'

rapidity and a total lack of digestion. As Lucy pointed out, it would have been perfectly easy to gather in the harvest, wash it in a strainer and proceed with the cake-making. No one would have been any the wiser, she felt sure, and would this not avoid a trip to the shops to get more ingredients? For obvious reasons we side-stepped this suggestion and I pulled myself together sufficiently to knock up one of my rather saggy chocolate sponges in the nick of time to save the day, and, we hoped, the 'blind dogs.'

Meanwhile, summer had arrived. Our large family of animals, with Michael Heselspine as leader of the pack, kept us fully occupied. Having Michael on the spot gave me a wonderful opportunity to take some photographs of a hedgehog being informal and relaxed. Ever good-natured and co-operative, he posed in front of various 'concocted' backdrops and sets. With a slightly bemused expression on his face, he sat obediently among my collection of china frogs and owls, agreed to being photographed pottering in our tasteful avocado bath, rather a favourite haunt of his, providing it is empty, and even submitted to posing, as it were, 'underwater' surrounded by sea-shells, starfish, and homemade sea creatures. He took it all in his stride, hardly batting a prickle when confronted by a rather fierce-looking plastic lobster.

Over the summer, other hedgehogs arrived to spend some time with us, mostly orphaned hoglets or just young inexperienced adults in need of care and attention. Betty Boothroyd and Edwina Currie, found abandoned in the nest, spent many weeks in our care, becoming quite tame and at ease in human company. I'd never actually looked after blind unweaned hoglets before, and caring for them was a full-time job. Food and warmth was what was needed most, and a warm hot-water bottle wrapped in an old towel was a great comfort to two tiny pricklies who were missing their mum.

We gave them baby milk in a small syringe, Lucy and I, administering it every three hours or so, with the two tiny hoglets lying contentedly on their backs in a nest of towelling. Goat's milk, diluted with a little water, is also excellent and very nourishing, but as no goat had so far managed to infiltrate our ranks, and with cow's milk being quite unsuitable, the baby milk more than filled the bill.

By four weeks, with their eyes now open, Edwina and Betty appreciated a proper box to sleep in, with hay and other suitable bedding provided. A nice shredded loo roll and some paper towels give both interest and warmth, as hoglets of this age have started to enjoy tearing things up and making 'dens.' By the time Edwina and Betty were up to a little gentle loo roll baiting, they were also becoming very partial to a 'big kid's diet', partaking noisily of scrambled egg, sloppy dog food and even a little gravy-soaked Hovis!

Taking on late 'autumn babies' is something of a commitment, as you have to feed them through the winter. I'd had two 'teenage' hogs under my wing the previous winter, both hopelessly underweight and doomed, as a late litter, not to get through hibernation. After they had been waited on hand and foot all winter, it would have been unthinkable just to turn them loose into the wicked world even if the weather had turned warmer.

A short period of rehabilitation is essential, and our two were encouraged to root round for themselves in a large outdoor run before we let them go. Lucy was a great help collecting worms, beetles, slugs and other natural delicacies and secreting them in suitable 'hidey-holes' inside the nursery pen so that the hoglets were obliged to forage for their supper.

As a rule, young hedgehogs adapt quite well to life back in the wild. I make a point of not releasing them during a very dry spell when liquid sustenance is hard to find, rather choosing a time, preferably at dusk when the weather is warm and moist and food is plentiful.

The vets never cease to be amazed that, considering all the years I've been keeping rabbits and guinea-pigs, I still seem incapable of getting my genders accurate. 'Humphreys' turn out to be Humphrettas, 'Georginas' have to change their names to George, 'Franks' to Francesca, and so on. A typical example of this involved Benjamin, a scrawny little wild-rabbit-coloured rabbit, purchased in a weak moment from a slightly suspect pet shop. Benjamin, a classic case of what Ian calls a 'C.R.I', or 'couldn't resist it', settled in nicely, put on weight and soon grew sleek and glossy. After three weeks it suddenly became abundantly clear that a rapid change of name was indicated. A splendid litter of nine multi-coloured babies appeared a couple of mornings later, and 'Benjamin' (no time to muck about with deed polls), instantly became Benjamina. When they were old enough, we distributed most of the litter amongst Lucy's school friends, but kept three, two boys, Clarence and Baldrick, and a delectable speckled girl christened Millicent, who went on to win some prizes, and later became a great buddy of Michael Heselspine's.

Where animals are concerned, I reckon I can cope with most eventualities, but mousetraps have got me licked. I hate them. The sight of a very small wood-mouse pursuing a runaway Malteser across our kitchen floor one morning enthralled me, and harbouring a passion, as I do, for small whiskery rodents, I find the setting of mousetraps and the administration of poison totally abhorrent.

An enchanting example of 'small and furry' was Mildred, a white mouse whom we had for two years. Everyone loved Mildred, including, so it seemed, a large cross-section of the local indigenous mouse population who began inviting themselves in droves with a view to socialising with Mildred through the bars of her cage. Deciding that our nice warm centrally heated kitchen was a distinct improvement on the chilly potting shed or great outdoors, they soon moved in 'en masse' and made themselves at home. The airing cupboard was the site chosen for the nomadic settlement, and I soon began to discover towels and sheets with holes chewed in them, and pillow cases that more closely resembled lace doilies.

The final straw came when I uncovered a nest of tiny pink babies curled contently inside my fur hat on the top shelf. Something had to be done, but, imagining the distress of the mother had she come and found her family gone, the hat stayed where it was until the babies were old enough to leave.

Quite apart from disliking what a mousetrap can do to a mouse, I'm not too keen on what it can do to my fingers. I'm hopeless at setting them, and particularly loathe those nasty metal ones with spikes that look like medieval instruments of torture. I can't describe the feeling of total betrayal I experience as I do battle with the odious objects, endeavouring to place a tempting piece of cheddar in the appropriate position, while struggling to get the evil metal bar at the correct angle. I was doing this one evening when I noticed Mildred observing me with some gravity from her cage on the kitchen counter. Quite

'Millicent and Michael are good chums…'

what she would have thought of me had she known I was setting up the means whereby to exterminate her friends and relations, I dread to think.

One has to admit that, if you really do have a mouse problem, traps, however grisly, are the answer. Mice have a tiresome habit of multiplying with alarming rapidity, and the damage they can do is horrendous. Even so, I have to force myself to open the airing cupboard door in the morning to check on the night's tally of pathetic little corpses.

My discovery of tights at the age of eighteen, when I finally realised that my legs and stockings were not compatible, was like a glorious new dawn. Discovering the humane mousetrap was even better! The humane mousetrap consists of a plastic tube, some six or seven inches long, into which a mouse can creep in search of a tasty tit-bit placed up the other end. These traps are designed a bit like lobster-pots; once the lobster, or, in this case, mouse, is in, it can't get out again, having released a small trap door which has closed behind it. The mouse, though probably suffering a mild dose of claustrophobia, is quite unhurt. While being of undeniable benefit both to the mouse and to my nerves, the humane mousetrap does have one drawback. What the hell do you do with the offending rodent once it is captured? Surely, you do not then administer the *coup de grâce*, as this would eliminate the reason for using the humane trap in the first place. It is just like the wombats all over again.

My personal solution to this knotty problem is to sneak furtively out under cover of darkness and release the prisoner either in the cornfield behind the house, if it is summer, or if it is on the chilly side, in the nice cosy hay barn belonging to a local farmer over the road. In either case, as Ian was swift to point out, such was the reputation of our three-star airing cupboard, that he could just visualise long columns of luggage-toting mice tramping slowly and purposefully back to our premises with a view to reclaiming squatters' rights.

As I have already stated, keeping four dogs in a smallish house in a supposedly tranquil cul-de-sac, can be, at best, a challenging experience. On the whole they are very good. Dear old Digger, the Border Terrier, has just celebrated his sixteenth birthday, sitting up at the table, a red bow on his tartan collar, to a Selkirk bannock, complete with blue icing and a candle. I've had Digger longer than any other dog and, though nearly blind and totally deaf, he still enjoys his grub and walkies. Though he recently passed his M.O.T. with flying colours, I know that, inevitably, he can't go on for very much longer. I'll know when the time comes to call a halt, I've done it so often before, but it never gets any easier. You have to do what's best for the animal and never mind your own feelings. I just thank heavens that I live in an age when we may decide when a much-loved pet has 'had enough' and enable that pet to pass on quickly, cleanly and with no pain.

I long ago made up my mind that, even if animals do not qualify for our heaven, they surely have a heaven of their own. I'm quite determined that, unless directed, like Orpheus, to the underworld, I shall inform the good St. Peter firmly but politely that, if it's humans to the right and Jack Russells and hedgehogs to the left, I intend to go left.

Basically, I think I am a reasonably easy-going type. However, I get absolutely hopping mad when I hear the more unsavoury sections of the population, such as football hooligans, badger-baiters, neo-Nazis and the like, described as 'behaving like animals'. Whoever heard of animals hurling petrol bombs or beating up old ladies for their meagre savings? I find this most offensive and unjust.

When you observe the behaviour of some of us humans, you wonder how we dare put up notices saying 'NO DOGS AL-LOWED' when, in many instances, the average dog (with the possible exception of the Jack Russell) behaves infinitely better then your average human. Nature has a natural dignity that we humans should endeavour to imitate. We could learn a great deal from animals if we only paused for a moment every now and then, to try.

Naturally our dogs all have names, in fact, all four have nicknames as well. Some less well adjusted dogs might find this muddling, but our four are quite *au fait*, and respond accordingly. Digger was so named because the very first thing he ever did the day I got him as an eight-week-old puppy was to head for the garden and dig up every single one of my newly planted daffodil bulbs. Then, of course, there is Mippy, who was actually Poppy when we first got her, but somehow Mippy suited better. Next is Inky, the black collie-cross (or cross collie, depending on the mood of the day). When we got her from the dog pound, she was rather uninspiringly called Kit. Lucy, then aged three, took one look and just said 'Inky', and so she has remained. Last is Bin-Bin, who was given her name for reasons I have already explained.

When in company or within possible earshot of the neighbours, we address our dogs by their standard names, it sounds so much more genteel, but when it's just us, and anything goes, we tend to go down-market a bit, especially if the family canines are being less than co-operative for any reason. When

102

this is the case, I regret to say that we lower the tone no end by addressing the doggies dear as the four 'Oi's'. Digger, as the eldest, being 'Oi' number one, and so on down to Bin-Bin, who is 'Oi' number four and easily the 'Oi' most regularly addressed as such, owing to a natural tendency towards 'Oi-ish' behaviour. Indeed, we have had to point out to her that as she was the last 'Oi' in, she would therefore be the first 'Oi' out in the event of serious canine misdemeanour. She was an 'Oi' for days on end after the recycled sultana episode, but I have to say, it is so much easier to say 'Oi' rather than 'get your face out of the ruddy bucket', or, 'after you with my best slippers', or whatever. Fortunately the four 'Oi's' don't appear to object to this basic form of address , and Mippy, who really qualifies as a full-time 'Oi', actually seems to like it.

Because of the size and variety of our private zoo, Ian and I do not manage to get away together very often. Weddings and funerals are a must, however, and it is on these occasions that a relay of kind neighbours come in and feed the other crea-tures, and we put the dogs into a local kennels. Digger is rather beyond this now, and we try, if we possibly can, to take him with us.

Inky and Bin-Bin tolerate the kennel regime, mope a bit, but soon adapt to boarding school life. Mippy, wouldn't you have guessed, adores it! She looks upon our local kennel rather as an up-market holiday camp, a sort of canine Butlins. While the others go all dejected and limp on arriving, Mippy takes on a new lease of life, leaps from the car, and without bothering to kiss us goodbye, rushes in to see if there are any old chums from last year in residence and suss out the menu and seating arrangements in the dining-room.

Christmas is an unbelievably expensive time for me. Apart from being an auntie seven times over, I am, oh horrors, also a great auntie seven times over too, and do quite like to give a few little gifts here and there. Besides this, Lucy, entering into the festive spirit, makes it her personal business to see that every single animal hangs up a stocking.

The sheer mental strain of having to remember what the goldfish had in their stockings last year so that history does not repeat itself this year, can be hard on the old nerves. Thankfully, Lucy arranges all stocking-filling now, though even she opts out when it has come to the stick insects. The dogs are relatively easy, 'chews' and biccies being easily wrapped and stashed away, but when it comes to hedgehogs, my mind goes completely blank. What, I ask myself, would you like to find in your stocking if you were a hedgehog? Obviously choices like slugs, snails, worms etc. are out at that time of year. This is probably just as well, as I don't terribly fancy the idea of gift-wrapping a soggy slug. One is really only left with the inevitable tin of dog food which can actually look quite seasonal, once wrapped in paper featuring jolly Santas and festive robins.

You may well wonder how on earth I manage to fit in any horse painting at all. The answer to this is that I don't really. I do what I can when I can, but it isn't easy. I long ago gave up all idea of painting horses from life, and now work entirely from photographs. This is infinitely less traumatic and means that I can work peacefully, Jack Russell permitting, at home in the kitchen within easy grabbing distance of a bowl of popcorn and with an Aled Jones or Luciano Pavarotti tape going in the background.

I did try painting horses from life when I first started out, but horses will *not* stand still, even in a head collar and on the end of a stout rope. All they want to do is come and see how you are getting on, have an infuriating habit of knocking over your easel, and invariably end up scoffing your last tube of burnt umber while standing squarely on your most expensive paint brush.

I do like to photograph the horse myself if it's humanly possible, though of course, this is impracticable if the equine is deceased, or alive and well but living in outer Mongolia. Should this be the case, you simply have to hope to heavens that the owners either have some suitable photos that you could work from, or are sufficiently handy with a box brownie to be able to take some. Painting horse portraits from other people's snaps can prove quite problematic, to put it mildly. Having to use a magnifying glass in order to tell if the small brown dot in the middle of a huge meadow is in fact a horse and not a rabbit, does not augur too well for a satisfactory portrait.

It never fails to amaze me how many D.I.Y. photographers send me photos of the prospective subject showing very little but muzzle and whiskers. This indicates that your request for a 'close-up' of the head has perhaps been taken a little too literally, and that the aspiring Beaton or Bailey has deliberately encouraged the animal to stand with its nose about three and a half inches from the camera lens. When I tell people that I paint horses, they all respond in a similar way by saying, 'Oh, do you do dogs?'. The answer to this is that 'No, I don't do dogs'. I did try for a while, but they all looked like horses, even the Jack Russells.

Though painting and writing are among my favourite pastimes, and tremendously satisfying, both are devilishly hard work and time-consuming. They can also be somewhat anti-social. I find that, when I'm deeply immersed in the task of capturing an equine likeness, everything else tends to come to a grinding halt. This is all very well, but if there are dogs to be walked, rodents to be cleaned out and a hedgehog to rub down, not to mention a husband and small daughter to be nurtured, things can get a little thwart. All this made worse by the fact that there is a half-finished Welsh Cob glaring at me from the easel!

As for writing, I find that keeping a pad of paper and a biro by the bed is a sensible way of capturing nocturnal flashes of literary inspiration. Rather like a hedgehog, my brain seems at its most astute round about three o'clock in the morning. Sitting bolt upright in bed at any time from midnight to four, and commencing to scribble furiously for the next three hours, is not entirely conducive to a tranquil night's sleep, either for me or for Ian. Luckily for me, he is wonderfully understanding about such things, and a heavy sleeper to boot, so that, on the whole, these spurts of manic scribbling during the silent watches, do not bring about too much marital discord. The most obvious drawback to this nocturnal jottery is that I tend to be a total zombie for the whole of the next day.

One equine commission that brought particular joy to me, and most especially to Lucy, was a head portrait that I did of a perfectly gorgeous little Dartmoor mare. She was jet black with huge liquid eyes and a wonderfully pretty head. Her owner, a lady well known as a breeder of top-class Dartmoors, was genuinely thrilled with the end result and promptly offered to lend us Corbie for the next two summers.

I seem to remember that, when I was Lucy's age, gymkhanas held no attraction, being rather too fast and furious for me, preferring as I did a gentle potter around the woods on a riding school hack. Even at that age I could not help but notice the change wrought in other small girls of my acquaintance when, dressed to kill in Harry Hall riding gear, they'd gather in the collecting ring ready for the various events. Hard hats clamped well down, jaws set in determination, they'd crouch in their saddles, riding crops at the ready, all set to do battle, while normally easy-going, level-headed mothers of would-be Olympic medallists, quite suddenly turned into frenzied viragos, yelling and screaming, one assumed, in an effort to goad their offspring to greater glory.

Lucy, unlike Mamma at the same age, felt that a little competitive riding might be fun. So, nothing daunted, I picked up a small second-hand trailer in reasonably good nick, and we proceeded to 'do' the gymkhanas. When first embarking on this venture, I had rather forgotten that Lucy, then only seven, was still quite firmly on the leading rein, for gymkhanas at any rate, and so it was that, clad in green wellies, Barbour and 'Country Life' felt trilby, so as not to be outdone by the other gymkhana-ing mums, I discovered, at the age of nearly fifty, a turn of speed I never knew I had.

There were small shows most weekends, and off we'd go, Corbie gleaming like a ripe blackberry, kind Ian having first introduced the trailer to the car for us, a job which I never did manage to achieve. I'd never driven a pony trailer in my life before, and found it slightly unnerving, glancing constantly in the mirror to see if Corbie was still with us. Reversing was utterly beyond my capability, so, unless Ian was there, I had to try to get through a whole show without having to go backwards.
I had to be 'rescued' several times, and once drove all the way to a show with the hand-brake of the trailer on. I couldn't understand why we arrived belching black smoke and smelling

like a rubber tyre factory on fire, or why poor Corbie staggered out of the box looking as though she'd knocked back three double whiskies along the way.

From early on, it was blatantly obvious to me that the rosettes went to those kiddies who could come up with the most athletic dads. Though some of the slimmer and more ambitious mothers did occasionally take to the field, most of them, noticeably those of more ample proportion, elected to bounce up and down on the touch-line and screech encouragement.

Though he had never been near a horse in his life before, Ian adapted with surprising ease and willingness. Being around six foot two, and long in the leg, he very soon proved formidable competition for those other fathers who came up against him. He positively hared up and down with Corbie thundering along behind on a string, Lucy, crouching Piggott-like in the saddle, yelling for him to slow down as the rest of the field were either half a mile behind or still in the starting stalls!

As Ian, seeking to preserve some semblance of dignity, had drawn the line at the clear round jumping, I found myself, green wellies and all, leaping over dozens of horrid little red and white jumps with, I may say, not inconsiderable flair. Even Lucy was impressed, especially as both Corbie and I somehow managed to achieve a clear round on most occasions. Lucy, with an eye to the main chance, noted that, for a pound a go, you could hurtle round the jumps as often as you liked, and decided that, as both Corbie and mum were neat little jumpers, this was an excellent chance to accumulate a sackful of nice colourful rosettes. Though willing to encourage my offspring in the pursuit of sporting excellence, I decided that, though none of the jumps was more than a foot high, three goes were more than enough.

This sentiment was echoed by one of the ring stewards who suggested, as tactfully as he could, that he felt that I was no longer, perhaps, of suitable age nor dimension for 'show jumping', and could he perhaps help out by taking Lucy round the jumps himself? I accepted his well-timed and kind invitation, and off he set. Though a 'bright young thing' of around 35, and skinny with it, he blotted his copybook by knocking three jumps flying and clocking up about twenty faults. Lucy needless to say, was not amused, and felt that despite all the odds, good old mum was definitely a better bet.

The following summer, we went through the whole palaver all over again, only this time, thank the Lord, Lucy was off the lead rein and able to fend for herself. 'Grimkhanas', as they were usually described by Ian, were actually quite fun. We had a crack at everything from the egg and spoon race to something rather mysterious called 'handy hunter'. Lucy enjoyed it all, and thanks to mum's ability with crêpe paper, paint and glue, did particularly well in the mounted fancy dress.

Meanwhile Michael Heselspine, not to be out-shone by the horse fraternity, was also to join the 'show-set' that summer. We took him to our local county show and put him in the most-unusual-pet class. The organisers were fearfully thrilled and observed that, over all the years, they had never had a hedgehog before. The judge appeared, a tweedy lady in a pork-pie hat and pink wellies, and eyed the array of unusual pets which included a rather smelly Jacob's sheep, a bored looking moth-eaten guinea-fowl, and a pale sad-looking frog in a Nescafé jar.

Michael, alerted by all the excitement and the close proximity of a somewhat noisy pipe band, unrolled and surveyed the scene

'With a much larger woolly "relative" ... '

with noticeable misgiving. Whether it was the cantankerous looking ferret parked next to him or the pipe band, his reaction was instant. Taking one look, he pulled down all the shutters and remained tightly curled and heaving with indignation for the rest of the class.

Lucy, clad in her new Hedgehog Preservation Society T-shirt, grinned cheerfully at the pork-pie hat and pink wellies, and apparently managed to convince her that Michael was indeed an example of hedgehog preservation at its best, for we won a blue rosette and repaired to the car in triumph, our prize-winning hog curled tightly in an empty Stork Margarine tub.

Michael Heselspine's next appearance in public was even more satisfactory, and won him further recognition. The annual old folk's party in the village hall brought invitations for Lucy to do a poem and for me to trot out a couple of my Joyce Grenfell monologues. After much persuasion, Lucy agreed to perform a poem called 'The Hedgehog', with Michael appearing along-side to add a bit of dramatic authenticity.

The day of the party arrived and we set out for the hall where some twenty local pensioners were eagerly anticipating tea and entertainment. All proceeded according to plan, and the old folk enjoyed their tea and settled back in comfy chairs for the floor show. Up got Lucy and gave quite a creditable rendering of her poem. Michael Heselspine, meanwhile, unknown to the old dears, was lurking furtively among a collection of Lucy's toy hedgehogs on a small table near the front of the stage, and stole the show completely by peering out from behind a large woolly 'relative', and grinning affably at the audience. His stage debut went down a treat, and he was the highlight of the afternoon.

'Michael Heselspine meets Quentin Hog…'

Several young hedgehogs came to stay over the summer, and I found that quite a lot of my time was taken up with hedgehog care and maintenance. Apart from Betty Boothroyd and Edwina Currie, we also acquired a very dehydrated little hog whom we christened Virginia Prickly-Bottomley. She was one of those hogs who just does not adapt to confinement or human proximity. Once she felt better she proceeded to devote all her time to trying to escape, climbing up and abseiling down the wire of her pen and rushing about with such agitation that, the moment I felt she was up to it, we took her to the large slug-infested meadow near the river and released her.

When visiting my hedgehog-mad friend, Irene, one day, I was intrigued to meet two adult hogs in residence at the time. Both were quite enormous and resembled prickly footballs rather than hedgehogs. Michael, who was with me, appeared quite fascinated and promptly started to anoint himself, emitting little hissing sounds and craning around to spread saliva over the prickles on his flank. No one really knows why hedgehogs perform this strange ritual, but on this occasion, I rather felt it must have been brought on by the sight of such outsize specimens of his breed. At the time of my visit, neither hog had acquired a name, so thinking to perpetuate the political line, we named them Arthur Scarquill and Quentin Hog.

Arthur and Quentin had both been successfully treated for maggot infestation. Using tiny metal tweezers, Irene had meticulously removed every one of the tiny pests. The one golden rule of hedgehog-keeping is that you must never leave uneaten food out during the daytime, especially in warm humid weather. Dishes of over-ripe dog food and other pungent delicacies are irresistible to hungry bluebottles which descend in droves, feast, then lay their eggs by way of a 'thank you'. Newly hatched maggots are desperately dangerous to hedgehogs: they attack the soft underparts, and, if not checked, can literally eat the unfortunate hog alive, burrowing into eyes, ears and mouth, and most horrendous of all, the poor little chap's rear end.

Apart from the work involved in caring for hedgehogs, there is the inevitable problem of expense. Michael is quite capable of polishing off half a tin of dog food most evenings. It is not so bad over the summer when you can while away a happy hour or so in the pursuit of natural food, but wintering young hogs who are unable to hibernate, can be a pricey amusement. A varied diet is essential to maintain a good level of health and vigour, and besides, your average hog most certainly appreciates the odd change of menu.

Having blotted my copybook with our local supermarket manager one day by informing him that the quite ghastly banshee wailing that emanated thunderously from the piped-music system was more akin to a hippopotamus suffering the latter stages of a strangulated hernia, than some supposedly world-famous female pop singer, I disgraced myself again the following week by collapsing in fits of unseemly mirth while bending over the frozen meat cabinet. It was simply the thought of actually having to make up my mind between a pound of minced beef for the hedgehog or a frozen chicken breast for hubby, that appealed to me. Such monumental decisions should never be taken lightly.

Doogie Douglas-Hamilton, another local hedgehog with parliamentary connections, was a rather lazy hog who came to stay with us while his owners treated themselves to a couple of weeks on the Costa. As he was particularly fond of eggs and equally partial to worms, I wondered if one might combine the

'About to tuck into Sunday lunch...'

two without having to scrape sticky egg yolk off Doogie's face yet again, I decided to try him on a nice worm omelette.

The recipe for this delicacy is quite simple and enables the diner to enjoy both eggs and worms without having the stress of chasing escaping worms all over the shop. First beat up your eggs with a tiny drop of diluted milk, allow to cook slowly in a small omelette pan over a low heat before adding half a dozen finely chopped worms. Doogie liked the look of his first omelette, fell to, and guzzled the lot, while Lucy, not too happy with this particular culinary project, felt that the S.S.P.C.A. might not take too kindly to the diced worm side of things.

Our freezer, apart from containing all the usual things like choc ices, frozen peas and bumper-sized packs of fish fingers, harbours several Tupperware containers full of mysterious little packages carefully wrapped in tin foil and bearing labels marked 'HEDGEHOG FOOD, HANDS OFF!' Ian, thinking to make himself a quick snack, has, on several occasions, mistakenly thawed out a pack containing diced lamb's liver and mince, or some such equally tempting selection of comestibles supposedly destined for Michael's high tea. Were the muddle to occur the opposite way round, a certain well-fed Erinacean of our acquaintance might well find himself enjoying some newly defrosted smoked salmon or prime rump steak at ten quid a go.

Michael is surely the only hedgehog in Scotland who enjoys four-star service at dinner time. Not only is his evening meal carried out to him on a tray, but he often gets two courses into the bargain. One can concoct a palatable soup out of liquidised leftovers which is a most acceptable starter. Michael approves of this no end, and slurps away appreciatively at his saucer before tackling the main course of the day. I have yet to think

'The Author with daughter Lucy, Mippy and Bin-Bin.' *Photo by Ian Horn.*

up a suitable dessert, but no doubt, that will come in time. Perhaps a little slug-flavoured ice cream or snail gâteau would go down well!

It is a bit like running a café for animals. The evening feeds take time, and I do feel just a little like a glorified waitress as I trot round hutches, cages and shed delivering the evening's 'nosh'. Apart from the usual things, hedgehogs like the occasional spoonful of sugar-free muesli over their meat, and perhaps a few peanuts as well. If you do serve up peanuts - and they are full of protein - for Lord's sake, chop them up as it is quite possible for a peanut to jam in the roof of a hedgehog's mouth causing great discomfort and even preventing the unfortunate hog from eating anything else.

It is comforting for me to know that I am not the only barmy female in the vicinity. My friend, Penny-up-the-road, is every bit as batty, especially where animals are concerned. I once dropped in to find her sitting in the kitchen reading a book, a small black cat draped round her neck and Beakly, the tame jackdaw, perched happily on her head. On the table beside her, grinning satanically, squatted a large pumpkin, ready, as it turned out, for the children's Hallowe'en party. I couldn't help but think that had she lived in times gone by, my friend Penny might well have been condemned as a witch, ending up either in the ducking-stool or, worse still, burnt at the stake.

Animals are wonderful natural clowns; dogs in particular have a superb knack of producing merriment and what-not with very little effort on their part. Once, when I was driving Lucy to school on a very frosty morning in November, we were treated to the beguiling sight of the entire population of our local hunt kennels perched on their potties in the roadside field used by the hunt for morning exercise and leg-cockery. Lucy was enchanted, and I had to admit that the sight of a whole pack of rather chilly looking foxhounds, ears flat, tails stuck rigidly out behind, emptying their tanks en masse, each with an expression of pained concentration on its face, was comical in the extreme. Lucy, who had been dolefully contemplating the probability of a maths test later that morning, was quite rejuvenated by the sight of the canine 'Relief of Mafeking'!

Enjoy your animals I say, but here a world of caution. Never allow yourself to get on first name terms with prospective Christmas dinners or Sunday lunches. I once got very chummy with a duck called Hitler, a bustling busy sort of chap who marched about the yard quacking orders not unlike a Nazi storm trooper on parade. The awful realisation that the excellent casserole served me for supper one evening by his owners was poor old Hitler accompanied by a pile of spuds and veggies, was devastating indeed, and my conscience pricked for weeks.

I think I learnt to trust animals from an early age. I can certainly remember nanny clucking disapprovingly as I tottered up to completely strange dogs to hug and deliver sloppy kisses upon unsuspecting but invariably receptive noses. Lucy showed early signs of similar tendencies, and as a toddler frequently introduced herself to strange quadrupeds of various shape and size. When she was about three, we went on a picnic with several other tinies and their Mums. All went well until the sun-drenched peace was suddenly shattered by the arrival of four large and very inquisitive black-faced sheep. Mums and tinies scattered leaving Lucy sitting fatly on the outspread car rug, sun-hat at a jaunty angle, bounteously handing out tuna-fish sandwiches and Penguin biscuits to the woolly invaders as though it was the daily norm.

There was really only one occasion that I remember being genuinely frightened by an animal. We were in a game reserve in South Africa, driving slowly along minding our own business, when, much to our horror, a fully grown and distinctly irritable-looking lioness detached herself from the bushes and approached the car. My brother, who was at the wheel, switched off the engine and we sat hardly daring to breath as the huge cat slowly and deliberately hauled herself up on the bonnet and with a loud grunt, lay down and glared at us through the windscreen. I was in the front passenger seat, and the sight of that huge feline licking her chops, not a foot from my face, with nothing but a thinnish sheet of glass between us, was alarming to say the least. Had she come over peckish and had a swipe at the windscreen with a massive paddy-paw, I'd have been a goner. Great therefore was my relief when she finally slid off the bonnet and padded nonchalantly off into the bush. I'd always quite liked pussy cats in fact, but that was something else.

I've been lucky, I've met animals from all over the world. I reckon there can't be that many middle-aged ladies around who have had the privilege of riding an ostrich in Africa, been bolted with round the pyramids by an over-enthusiastic camel, and happily submitted to having her face almost entirely denuded of make-up by a London Zoo giraffe with a three-foot tongue. Surprisingly, I've only ever been bitten badly twice in my life, so far at any rate, once by a menopausal corgi and once by a mole whom I apprehended pottering myopically around on my aunt's grass tennis court when I was about eight. In that instance, I dropped the unfortunate mole, who had bitten my finger, fainted dead away, and was carted off to hospital. In fact, no lasting damage was done, and in both cases it was entirely my own fault that I was bitten. The defaulters were

'Lucy having a "close encounter of the prickly kind..." '
Photo by Gordon Lockie.

quickly forgiven and, on the whole, I have got on pretty well with all my many friends over the years.

With my life having been so full of animals from as far back as I can remember, and being so acutely aware of just how much pleasure and companionship they have brought me, I honestly find it more or less impossible to imagine life without animals. Having been one of five children, I also find it hard to imagine what it must be like to be an only child. Without the fellowship of brothers or sisters, Lucy, growing up, as she is, surrounded by a variety of creatures, finds fun and friendship, merriment and learning. She is seldom bored, for there are always things to be done, young hedgehogs to coddle, dogs to groom and throw a ball for, ponies to ride, rabbits to be cleaned out and fed; the list is endless, and it is a great pleasure for me to see her growing up with the same affinity to animals as did I. Our pets are lucky, all are wanted and loved, and in return, give us endless interest, much pleasure and, not least of all, a time of laughter.

THE END